HOW CAN *i* SERVE?

NAVIGATING LEADERSHIP AND BUILDING COMMUNITIES

FEATURING THE CONSTELLATION EFFECT: A NEW VISION FOR LEADERSHIP

WADIA AIT HAMZA

Book Cover by Christie Borely

ISNB: 978-1-83556-361-8 eBook

ISBN: 978-1-83556-362-5 Papeback

ISBN: 978-1-83556-363-2 Hardback

Disclaimer:

This book is the result of a collaborative effort involving my personal experiences, insights, and the support of dedicated editors, friends, family, and artificial intelligence (AI) tools. Throughout the writing process, AI was utilized to assist in redrafting certain parts, refining ideas, and helping to shape concepts for enhanced clarity. Additionally, the expertise of editors played a significant role in polishing the manuscript and ensuring coherence and readability. While much of this book stems from my own journey, some sections reflect a collective effort, Kamal enriched by thoughtful input and feedback. I am especially grateful to Marie, Laila, and Brahim for their invaluable support throughout this process.

This collaboration also demonstrates how, when used thoughtfully, technology and human expertise can work together to support creativity and productivity while preserving the authenticity of the author's voice and experiences.

To Aylan & Solal,
you are the reason I believe in the future.
May you always walk through life with integrity,
kindness, and courage

CONTENTS

ACKNOWLEDGMENTS

Writing this book has been one of the most personal and humbling journeys of my life. It would not have been possible without the support, guidance, and encouragement of many remarkable individuals who have walked alongside me—each a star in the constellation that shaped this work.

First and foremost, I am deeply grateful to my family.

To my parents, Fanida and Mohamed—thank you for instilling in me the values of humility, service, and integrity. Your quiet leadership, lived with grace and conviction, continues to guide my every step.

To my siblings, Ghizlane, Rida, and Laila—thank you for being my anchors and my rockstars.

And to Marie, my partner in life and in purpose—this book simply wouldn't exist without you. Your unwavering support, sharp insight, loving patience, and belief in me during the hardest and brightest of days have shaped not only these pages but also the person I've become. Thank you for walking beside me, challenging me, holding space for me, and reminding me of what truly matters. This book is as much yours as it is mine.

To the countless Shapers, Young Global Leaders, Global Leadership Fellows (2013 cohort), and community leaders I've had the privilege of working with—thank you. You've shown me what it truly means to lead with heart, to listen deeply, and to build something greater than ourselves. A special recognition to the Moroccan Shapers—our endless conversations on leadership, service, and purpose continue to fuel my strength and inspire my journey.

To Professor Klaus Schwab—thank you for believing in the power of young people and for offering me a platform to grow, lead, and serve. I am deeply honored by your contribution of the foreword to this book. Your vision has inspired a generation, and I'm proud to be part of that legacy.

To my colleagues, mentors, and friends at the World Economic Forum and beyond—thank you for expanding my perspective and encouraging me to lead with both head and heart.

To my former line managers and colleagues who've left a lasting impact on me—Robert Burgess, Sanae Lyamouri, Marie Claude Azzouzi, Yemi Babington-Ashaye, and Adrian Monck—thank you for your trust and for the lessons that have stayed with me.

To my Al Akhawayn University community—thank you for shaping the early chapters of my leadership journey.

To Dr Abdellatif Bencherifa, Dr Driss Ouaouicha, and Dr Charif Belfekih—thank you for your leadership and unwavering support.

To Professor John Shoup, Professor Eric Ross, Professor Naceur Amakhmakh, Professor Brahim Boussouab, and Professor Abdelkrim Merzouki—thank you for your mentorship, support and trust.

To Abdesamad Fatmi—thank you for opening the door to leadership and for seeing potential in me before I ever saw it in myself.

To the unforgettable 011 cohort—thank you for rocking the university with your energy, laughter, and unwavering support.

To Khikhiz—Abdellah Abouessaid, Amine Aboussaid, Brahim Ait Ouzineb, Imad Abdeljaouad, Mounir Belcaid, and Mouad

Baha—thank you for your friendship, loyalty, and the lessons you didn't even know you were teaching.

To the many friends whose presence and support still resonate deeply—thank you. It's hard to name everyone here, but you know who you are. You've each contributed to who I am today, and I will always be grateful for the campus life we shared.

To my lifelong friends—those with whom every conversation is an exchange, a reflection, a learning— Hamadi Aít Hamza, Younes Belmaachi, Iguimdrane Nour-Eddine, Kamal Kimaoui, Zakaria Zrari—thank you for your enduring friendship and the wisdom you've shared along the way.

A heartfelt thank you to the editors, early readers, and thought partners who helped shape this manuscript. Your guidance brought clarity during moments when the words felt out of reach.

And lastly, to you—the reader—thank you for picking up this book with curiosity and intention. May it serve as a mirror, a guide, and a gentle reminder that leadership is not about standing above others, but standing with them.

Together, we are the constellation.

With gratitude,

Wadia

FOREWORD

By Professor Klaus Schwab
Founder, World Economic Forum

In 1971, I founded the World Economic Forum with the conviction that business should serve all stakeholders—customers, employees, communities, and shareholders. This stakeholder concept has guided our mission to improve the state of the world. Over the decades, this vision led to the creation of initiatives like the Forum of Young Global Leaders in 2004 and the Global Shapers Community in 2011, empowering young leaders to address global challenges and shape a more inclusive, sustainable, and resilient future.

As we transition into the Intelligent Age, leadership must evolve. Rapid advancements in artificial intelligence, digitalization, and global interconnectivity are reshaping the world. Leaders today must demonstrate a unique blend of wisdom, resilience, and adaptability. I define these qualities through five essential dimensions. Soul is the moral compass that grounds leadership in values and ethics. Brain is the ability to think strategically and anticipate the ripple effects of change. Heart represents the emotional intelligence necessary to build trust and foster inclusion. Muscles are the capacity to execute bold ideas and turn vision into tangible impact. Nerves embody the courage to navigate uncertainty and stand firm in the face of adversity. These qualities are not abstract ideals but concrete imperatives for today's leaders—especially for those working to build and sustain communities that drive real impact.

This book, How Can i Serve?, explores the evolving nature of leadership and community-building in an increasingly interconnected and rapidly changing world. It examines how leadership is shifting from hierarchical authority to a more collaborative and service-oriented model. Drawing on both personal experience and broader societal trends, the book offers a roadmap for those who seek to create meaningful impact through collective action and trust-building.

What makes this book unique is its perspective on leadership as a constellation effect—where individual stars shine brightly on their own, but true transformation happens when they align to form something greater than the sum of their parts. It underscores the power of community-driven leadership, demonstrating that complex challenges are not solved in isolation but through interconnected efforts, shared purpose, and collective action. Just as a constellation guides travelers in the night, strong communities illuminate the path forward, creating lasting impact through collaboration and trust.

How Can i Serve? is a must-read for current and aspiring leaders, community organizers, policymakers, educators, and professionals navigating the complexities of leadership in their own fields. I invite them to reflect on their role in this journey. Readers will benefit from this book by gaining insights into how leadership can be reimagined for today's world. It offers practical strategies and thought-provoking reflections on how individuals and organizations can cultivate leadership that is not about standing above others but about standing with them.

By embracing a more inclusive and collaborative approach, readers will be better equipped to navigate challenges, inspire change, and build communities that thrive in the face of uncertainty.

INTRODUCTION

Writing this book wasn't something I planned, let alone dreamed of. Family, friends, and colleagues have often urged me to share the lessons, insights, and stories that shaped who I am today. "You should write a book," they'd say—at conferences, in meetings, especially when speaking to youth leaders. Their encouragement was genuine, but the idea always felt daunting, almost unreachable to me. How could I, someone who never considered writing a natural strength, put my idea into words?

Public speaking came with its challenges, but over time, I learned to manage the fear, quiet the imposter syndrome, and step into moments confidently. Speaking feels manageable, shaped by the energy of the audience, the rhythm of a conversation, and the immediacy of connection. A book, though, is something else entirely. It's still, permanent, and deliberate. Writing demands a kind of commitment that leaves no room for the comfort of spontaneity. It requires focus, discipline, and time—not just hours or days, but the kind of time you can only give when you're ready to slow down and truly reflect.

I grew up watching my father pour himself into his books, one after another. I saw the hours he spent at his desk, the quiet determination etched into his every move, and the patience it took to bring ideas to life in words. His last book was an autobiography, a testament to his resilience and a legacy my siblings and I encouraged him to leave behind. It captured the meaning of his journey—something tangible, something future generations could hold onto. I admired his ability to turn his life into a story worth telling. But me? I never thought I had a story like that, at least not one that could stand beside his.

Even after leaving the World Economic Forum, I found myself invited to speak again and again—business leaders in London, youth gatherings in Morocco, and conferences in Switzerland. At first, I shrugged it off as an extension of the work I'd been doing. But then, I started to wonder: *could there be something in my journey, in the lessons I've lived, that others genuinely found valuable?* Perhaps the insights I've gained from building and leading communities in some of the world's most diverse and complex settings were worth preserving after all.

The turning point came during one of the most challenging chapters of my life. A perfect storm of professional setbacks, family struggles, and an unexpected accident left me immobilized—both physically and emotionally. With two broken hands, I couldn't do much except pause and reassess everything. It was in this forced stillness that a request came my way: a proposal for a new initiative centered on leadership and community building. I began drafting ideas, with my spouse helping me organize my scattered thoughts, and something unexpected happened. As I designed the proposal, I realized I wasn't just creating a proposal—I was outlining the principles and values that had shaped my journey.

During that time, I also picked up *The Servant* by James Hunter, a book that completely reframed how I viewed storytelling. Its simplicity and honesty reconciled me with the idea that I didn't need to be perfect to narrate my story. That realization was a revelation. So, I went back to the interviews and podcasts I gave during the last years, reviewed the articles I wrote, relooked at the proposals I designed, and transformed everything into something bigger: the blueprint for this book. What started as a response to a client's request evolved into a reflection on servant leadership, a guide to community building, and a story I finally felt ready to share.

That moment of realization—the decision to turn scattered ideas into a structured narrative—was both daunting and exhilarating. As the pieces began to fall into place, I saw this book not just as a reflection of my journey but as an offering. It was my chance to capture the lessons I've learned, the challenges I've faced, and the moments of growth that shaped my approach to leadership and community building. Most importantly, it was an opportunity to share these insights with others who might find themselves navigating similar paths.

This book is meant for anyone who wants to understand what it means to lead from a place of purpose, empathy, and humility. Whether you're a young leader, an established professional, or simply someone interested in building communities, I hope my journey provides both inspiration and practical insights. My aim is to offer a roadmap for those who seek to engage meaningfully in their organizations, volunteer networks, or professional communities, helping them build something lasting and impactful.

The core philosophy of this book is servant leadership. It's a model that emphasizes service over command and empowerment over control. Servant leadership isn't a management technique—it's a way of life. It's about creating spaces where everyone's voice matters, where each person is empowered to bring their best self forward. In this sense, the book is both a testimony to and a guide for those who believe in the transformative power of leading with humility and respect.

This journey will unfold in several parts. First, I'll walk you through the early stages of my life, sharing the foundational lessons that shaped my leadership and community-building approach. You'll see how my work evolved over time, particularly within the Global Shapers Community—a network of young leaders from around the world dedicated to making a positive impact. This part is less about instruction and more about immersion; it's a chance to experience the challenges, victories, and nuances of working within a diverse, global community.

As we move forward, the book delves into the heart of servant leadership, exploring the qualities that make this approach not only effective but necessary in today's world. In a time of rapid change and increasing complexity, leaders who prioritize service, empathy, and humility are better equipped to create meaningful connections and foster sustainable growth. I hope to illustrate how servant leadership is not just an ideal but a practical path to building communities that thrive on shared purpose and collective impact.

From there, the focus will shift toward curating communities—an art that requires careful attention to culture, structure, and purpose. Drawing on my experience mainly with the Global Shapers Community, I'll highlight the elements that I believe are essential for leaders to consider when nurturing communities, from establishing trust to fostering inclusivity. These chapters are designed to provide a more in-depth look at the specific strategies and methodologies I've found effective in creating vibrant, resilient communities.

As you progress in the book, we will explore the evolving landscape of community leadership, delving into the emerging challenges and opportunities that leaders will need to address. In an era marked by unprecedented connectivity yet profound division, the ability of leaders to bridge gaps and foster genuine connections has never been more critical. Finally, I'll dwell into the concept of The Constellation Effect—the central metaphor of this book that encapsulates the power of interconnected leadership and collective purpose. True leadership isn't about one individual at the center; it reaches its fullest potential when people unite, each bringing their own strength to form a collective force that thrives in service of something greater than themselves.

Ultimately, this book is a guide to servant leadership and community building through my journey. We all have privileges in life, and while they shouldn't be a source of shame, not using them for a greater purpose should be. I hope these stories and insights inspire you to reflect on how you can use your own experiences and strengths to create positive change. As you embark on it with me, I invite you to see the potential within each community, each interaction, and each moment of connection. This book is not about leadership alone but about a vision for a future where we all play a part in lighting the way forward, together. It's a mix of lessons, methodologies, stories, and takeaways, all designed to inspire and equip you with the tools you need to navigate the complexities of leadership and community building. I hope that by the end of this journey, you'll see how powerful servant leadership can be—not just as a concept, but as a way of creating lasting, meaningful change.

PART 1:

THE JOURNEY OF LEADERSHIP AND COMMUNITY

CHAPTER 1:
NEW VISION FOR LEADERSHIP: THE CONSTELLATION EFFECT

"No single star can light the night sky. Leadership is about the pattern we form, not the brightness we claim."
– Wadia Ait Hamza

When I gaze up at the night sky, I marvel at the beauty of each star shining brightly on its own. Yet, as I contemplate them, I am reminded that their true brilliance emerges when they come together to form a constellation—a pattern of light greater than the sum of its parts. This metaphor embodies my philosophy of leadership. True leaders do not seek to shine alone; they strive to weave connections, ensuring that their teams and communities become constellations of talent, purpose, and collective brilliance. The real magic of leadership lies not in individual radiance, but in the luminous networks we create together. I've shared this idea publicly in the Young Global Leaders Summit in 2023 in Geneva, Switzerland. The idea of standing before a room full of influential people was daunting yet replete with potential. Standing backstage and rehearsing the speech in my head was a lonely feeling; however, thinking of the other stars in the room made me excited. I didn't see just a collection of individuals. What struck me was how these stars, when aligned with a shared purpose, could create a unified picture of collective brilliance. A community.

The constellation analogy has stayed with me throughout my career, but I must confess, not as clear as it is right now. It's a metaphor I've carried into every team, every association, and every community I've been a part of, particularly the Global Shapers Community and the Forum of Young Global Leaders, which I had the honor to lead. Leadership is not about one person standing out, but how we all come together to make a lasting impact. It's about having a "star team," not just a "team of stars." Everyone has strengths, but connecting and working toward a common goal is the real power.

I had the chance to interact many times with Jack Ma, co-founder of Ali Baba, as he was a board member of the Global Shapers Community. One day, during an annual meeting in Davos with the Global Shapers, he told us something that has stuck with me until now: "My job is to make smart people work together, and if smart people can work together, then it's easy to believe in the vision." This notion reminds me of every time I stand before a summit audience full of smart people who shine in their own way: *to lead successfully, it's to lead a constellation, not to lead stars, each shining alone.* It's also not about being the brightest but about guiding others to shine together.

This idea became even more meaningful when I started working with the Global Shapers Community. Each hub in the Global Shapers Community operates independently, including its leadership and even its own logo. The curators, the leaders of these hubs, only serve for a one-year mandate. Their task is not only to lead but to think about the continuity of the hub, to ensure that their leadership helps leave a legacy. In this environment, I saw the power of the constellation effect—people working together, guided by a shared vision, each contributing their unique strengths.

Am I doing this right? I would sometimes ask myself, especially when everything felt chaotic. But I always came back to the same answer: leadership is not about controlling every piece; it's about creating a space where people feel valued and heard, where their contributions matter.

One of my most profound experiences with this collective leadership approach came during a crisis. It was during the summer of 2021 that the situation in Afghanistan was unravelling quickly, and the Taliban were taking over. A little over half a hundred Global Shapers were in danger because of their affiliation with us, an international organization, and we had to do something. There wasn't time for slow, deliberate decision-making. What happened next was one of the most incredible displays of community action I've ever witnessed. Community members from different countries came together, working tirelessly to aid those affected by the crisis.

I remember the calls and late-night messages. People were exhausted, but no one wanted to stop. Something deeper drove everyone—a shared sense of purpose that pushed us to keep going. No one was leading this effort; the same goal united everyone.

In such moments, I didn't have to ask people to act—they knew what needed to be done. This wasn't a team of individuals waiting for orders; this was a constellation in motion. Each star moved in harmony with the others, driven by a joint mission. And the results were far more significant than anything one could have achieved alone. The emotional connection and the trust we had built allowed us to do more than help those in need; we showed what's possible when people come together with intention.

I began reflecting on how leadership and communities are intertwined during this time. I would ask myself if some other models or frameworks could make a difference. But every time, I came back to the same thought: the power lies in the collective. We were not saving Afghanistan alone but doing what we could together. The situation demanded trust, collaboration, and unity, transcending borders and individual efforts. I'll share more about how this story unfolded later in the book.

Working with the Global Shapers and the Young Global Leaders communities brought these values into sharp focus. I saw firsthand how trust, empathy, respect, and inclusivity became the foundation for everything we accomplished. Without these cornerstones, it's nearly impossible to build a genuine community. Trust allows people to open up and feel safe enough to share their ideas, hopes, and fears. It's that trust that binds a group together, making it stronger.

During every project or initiative I worked on, I always tried to bring diverse voices together to tackle the issue. It wasn't just about logistics or who had the best strategy. What always makes an impact is the trust we have in each other. Each person had to know they had a place at the table. Every voice, no matter how different, should be heard and respected. That's how we always moved forward—not by following one leader, but by leaning on each other and respecting the unique perspectives each person brought, underscored by empathy and genuinely understanding the struggles and backgrounds of the people we worked with. When you lead with empathy, you make room for everyone's story. You start to see the bigger picture—not just as a collection of challenges to be solved but as a network of human experiences that need to be understood.

One evening, I received a video call from a Shaper from the Caracas Hub in Venezuela. I picked up the call but couldn't see anything. Network failure? Not at all. I could hear him loud and clear. I could listen to the voices of many people in the background but couldn't see who. To my surprise, the full Caracas Hub was gathering in the dark amid electricity failure in the whole country. They were adamant about holding the curators' elections within our deadline, even in the harshest social, economic, and political conditions. I was speechless in the face of the collective power of a hub, standing against the repression of the government. In a quiet moment, I started thinking about how far we had come. We weren't just working on a project or ensuring our governance was respected but building something more significant. It was as if each person, each voice, was a thread in a larger tapestry, and our task was to weave those threads together into something solid and beautiful.

Inclusivity was another critical pillar. I always believed that everyone must feel included for a community to thrive. That means ensuring that every voice—regardless of background, gender, or status—has a place in the conversation. At the Global Shapers, we worked hard to make this a reality. It wasn't always easy. There were moments when I questioned whether we were succeeding in this effort, such as during Black Lives Matter, when some members doubted our community's diversity and actions. But then I would witness the power of inclusivity, seeing people who might not have spoken up in other spaces take the lead to voice their opinions, run sessions, and launch projects. Their ideas weren't just heard—they were celebrated and acted upon.

But these values—trust, empathy, respect, and inclusivity—aren't just abstract ideals. They're lived experiences that shape how a community functions. At our gatherings, these values were our guiding principles. We took the time to truly listen to one another, supporting each other on a deep, personal level. It wasn't just about the work we were doing; it was about how we were doing it—together.

At one of the forums held for MENA Summits in Jordan, we had a particularly intense session where people from very different backgrounds and cultures were debating the sensitive issue of Palestine and Israel. We were discussing whether a meeting with Shimon Peres, former Israeli President, would be an occasion to discuss the political deadlock with young Arab Shapers. Some saw it as an opportunity to speak truth to power and face him, and some saw it as giving him a platform he didn't deserve. Emotions ran high, and it was clear that not everyone agreed. However, what stood out was the respect everyone maintained throughout the discussion. Even when there were disagreements, people communicated with care and listened to understand, not just to respond. That's what made the difference that day. Respect allowed us to navigate challenging conversations without losing the trust we had built. The meeting didn't take place in the end, but everyone grew with our discussion.

I remember stepping out of the meeting room, and as I walked toward the Dead Sea, the faint scent of saltwater in the breeze and the sight of the serene, glistening surface ahead seemed to mirror the tranquility I felt within. *This is how communities grow more robust*. It wasn't about avoiding conflict but facing it head-on with a commitment to empathy and respect. Everyone had something valuable to say, and we didn't shy away from difficult conversations. That meeting was a reminder that real progress often comes from the most challenging moments, and it's in those moments that communities grow closer and more resilient.

Ensuring diversity of thought wasn't something I ever took lightly. It was clear that real innovation comes when different perspectives are brought together. Throughout my career, I prioritized getting those diverse voices into the room, whether by consciously selecting a team from different backgrounds or ensuring that everyone had a chance to speak up. At the World Economic Forum, this became even more important. We were dealing with issues that affected the entire globe, and our discussions needed to include people from various industries, regions, and walks of life. It wasn't just about checking boxes or meeting quotas—it was about creating an environment where every voice was heard and people felt empowered to share their unique ideas.

This was especially true when listening to young people and underrepresented voices. I realized early on that these groups often have the most innovative solutions. They see the world differently, and their ideas can challenge the status quo in ways that more established voices might overlook. In many ways, they're the ones who push the boundaries and ask the tough questions that need to be asked. Ensuring these voices had a place at the table wasn't just important—it was essential to our work.

As a Global Shaper, I was honored to receive an invitation to apply for the inaugural cohort of Shapers attending the Africa Summit in Addis Ababa, Ethiopia, in 2011. Unfortunately, prior commitments prevented me from applying, but what I later discovered left a profound impression on me. Securing a space for Shapers at such a high-level meeting was no small feat. It was made possible by the visionary leadership of the World Economic Forum's Founder, Klaus Schwab, and the Africa Director at that time, Elsie Kenza. Their belief in the value of young voices broke through skepticism and resistance from those who questioned the inclusion of youth in such prestigious settings.

Many doubted whether young people belonged at a table traditionally reserved for seasoned leaders. The idea of a Shaper speaking at such an event was met with even more resistance. Yet, the Global Shapers team under the leadership of David Aikman persisted. Yemi Babghington Ashaye, deputy head at that time, fought to ensure that a Shaper would ask a question during the closing plenary—a moment shared with many Heads of State. When the time came, the Shaper posed a question that was both bold and poetic: "What kind of disease takes hold of some people that they cannot leave their seats after their mandate ends?" The question was masterfully crafted—pointed enough to address the unspoken truth in the room, yet neutral enough to avoid offending anyone directly. It was a courageous act of speaking truth to power, shining a spotlight on an uncomfortable issue no one else dared to voice and the importance of having young people at the table.

That moment was more than just a question. It set a precedent—a lasting legacy for young voices to be heard at the forum's events. From that point forward, Shapers earned their place at the table, not as mere participants but as essential contributors to the conversations shaping our world.

Building a truly inclusive environment goes beyond just gathering a diverse set of voices; it requires us to engage those voices meaningfully. As Verna Myers so powerfully argues: diversity is being invited to the dance, inclusion is being asked to dance, equity is about how much space you have on the dance floor, and belonging is about who gets to choose the music. True belonging means that people feel not just welcomed but valued, that they can bring their full selves without hesitation or fear of judgment. When every person in the room feels they're part of shaping the environment, we create a community where ideas flow freely, collaboration deepens, and innovation thrives. It's about more than inviting people into the room—it's about creating a space where everyone feels they are essential contributors rather than mere participants.

One of my hardest lessons is balancing when to lead from the front and when to step back. In the early days of my career, I was told, "Trust is good, but control is better." Being a good leader meant being involved in every decision, every step of the way. I had to prove myself by showing that I could handle everything. However, over time, primarily through my work with the Global Shapers and through the Global Leadership Fellows Program of the World Economic Forum, I realized that authentic leadership often means letting others take the lead. It's about trusting the people around you to own their work and the community's growth.

This wasn't an easy shift for me. Stepping back means letting go of control. There's always that fear: *What if things don't go as planned? What if the direction changes?* But I learned that you don't need to control every detail when you create a strong foundation built on trust, respect, and shared values. The team or the community will find its way, and often, they'll exceed your expectations.

The day I realized I had done my job as a leader for the Global Shapers team came under the most unexpected circumstances. In January 2022, I learned that I needed surgery for a hernia. The pain was unbearable, making it impossible for me to walk, and I knew I had to step away—something no leader finds easy. I was told I'd need at least two months to recover after the surgery, and the thought of being unable to contribute weighed heavily on me. But at that moment, I had no choice but to trust my team completely. Without a shadow of a doubt, I knew they could make decisions, navigate challenges, and drive every aspect of managing our community. So, I let go. I relinquished control, trusting in the leadership and strength I had helped cultivate in each of them. At first, it felt unnatural—like leaving behind a part of myself. Letting go of control wasn't easy; it meant confronting my fear that things might fall apart without me. Emotionally, I oscillated between relief and anxiety, constantly questioning whether I had done enough to prepare my team.

My daily routine changed drastically. Instead of managing endless emails, meetings, and calls, I found myself focusing on small, simple moments—physical therapy, reading, and rediscovering the luxury of rest. I had to spend at least seven hours each day lying on my bed, not counting nighttime sleep. The stillness forced me to reflect deeply on my role as a leader and the importance of trusting others. Meanwhile, I stayed updated on my team's progress from afar, resisting the temptation to intervene and respond to emails, marveling at how they rose to every challenge. This experience not only strengthened my confidence in their abilities but also reminded me of the transformative power of letting go—an essential lesson in leadership that I might not have fully embraced otherwise.

The two months of recovery passed more smoothly than I had anticipated. Aside from the physical pain and the sense of isolation, the only call I received was for one urgent matter—when the war in Ukraine broke out, requiring critical decisions. Even then, they had it under control. Every other detail, every task, every challenge—they handled it all seamlessly.

During those quiet days, as I watched from the sidelines, a profound realization dawned on me: they didn't need me anymore. And that's when I knew I had fulfilled my role as their leader—not because I was actively guiding them, but because I had empowered them to lead themselves. That is, after all, the true essence of leadership—not creating followers, but nurturing and equipping others to become leaders.

My cultural background has played a significant role in shaping my leadership style. Growing up in Morocco, the community was at the heart of everything. I was taught from a young age that we are responsible for ensuring our community's needs are met. Back in the little mountainous village in Morocco, hospitality is more than just being polite—it's a way of life. You welcome others with open arms, whether they are friends, family, or strangers. That idea of making people feel welcome and included has influenced how I build communities. Leadership, to me, is about service.

Humility has been a guiding principle throughout my journey. I've learned that the most influential leaders are willing to listen and learn, not just lead. Leadership is not about having all the answers or being the most thoughtful person in the room. It's about being open to the ideas and experiences of others and recognizing that leadership is a continuous learning process. There have been many moments in my career where humility has grounded me. When I didn't know the answer, I wasn't afraid to admit it. I would turn to my team and say, "I need your help." And it's in those moments of vulnerability that the real magic happens. When a leader shows humility, it invites collaboration. It shows others that their input is valued and that they are part of the solution.

I've also learned that humility is about being a follower, even when you're the leader. Sometimes, stepping back and allowing someone else to lead is your best decision. Leadership isn't about always being in control—it's about knowing when to let others guide the way. This was especially true during my time at the World Economic Forum. For every event or summit that the team had to host, someone from the team would be in charge. This would be our new boss and we would follow her/his lead. Watching team members step up, take risks, and grow into their potential was one of the most rewarding parts of my work. It wasn't about me leading—it was about them finding their path.

These experiences taught me that interdependence is essential in solving complex global challenges. No one can do it alone. It is a constellation— with each star shining, creating something far more powerful and beautiful when they come together. This is the kind of leadership I strive to embody and cultivate. It's not about being the brightest star but bringing others together to create a constellation that lights up the sky.

Each experience and challenge has strengthened my faith in this metaphor. Whether collaborating with diverse teams worldwide, spearheading a global initiative, or tackling daily obstacles, the constellation approach has continuously guided me. It emphasizes the importance of collective strength and the understanding that together, we are more formidable than alone. This reflects the core of my leadership journey—anchored in trust, humility, and the conviction that we can attain remarkable feats when united.

CHAPTER 2:
THE ROOTS

"You may encounter many defeats,
but you must not be defeated."
– Maya Angelou

The seeds of leadership were planted in me early, growing from my family's roots and the environment I was raised in. My childhood in Rabat, the capital of Morocco, was full of adventure, learning, and an awareness of our collective values. Originally from Kelaat M'gouna, my family frequently travelled between Rabat and the country's south-eastern parts, which allowed me to experience Morocco's incredible diversity. Whether it was the towering High Atlas Mountains or the waves of the Atlantic Ocean, the land always seemed alive.

It was more than just geography, though. The people we met, the stories they shared, and the kindness exchanged between neighbors, even in the smallest villages, left a deep impression on me. My father, Mohamed Ait Hamza, played a critical role in shaping my understanding of what it means to lead. His work as a geography university professor took him across the diverse landscapes of Morocco, from the towering peaks of the Atlas Mountains to the sprawling plains and vibrant coastal cities. Yet, his heart was always tied to his roots in Amejgag, where he was born, a village of around 1,500 people nestled in the rugged beauty of the High Atlas Mountains, near Mount Ighil M'goun—the second-highest peak in Morocco, rising majestically to 4,071 meters. Just 40 kilometers away from the south of Amejgag lies Kelaa M'gouna, the town where he grew up, famously known as the "Valley of Roses" for its flourishing rose fields and celebrated annual festival. In these serene yet resilient places, the spirit of community was not just a tradition but the very foundation of survival amidst the breathtaking yet demanding terrain.

My father's story is one of resilience and perseverance. He grew up in a place where life was anything but easy. Survival in Amejgag, and later in Kelaat M'gouna, required everyone to pitch in, work together, and care for one another.

I vividly remember him taking me as a child to the tribal celebration of the wheat harvest in Amejgag—a magical moment that remains etched in my memory. The entire village would come together to help with the final stages of the harvest, a joyous tribute to community and sustenance. The earthy aroma of freshly cut wheat filled the air, mingling with the rhythmic sound of mules circling the threshing plots, their steady steps separating the grains from the stalks. The melodic voices of women singing poetry wove through the air, adding an almost sacred rhythm to the day.

As children, we would line up eagerly, our hands outstretched in anticipation. The adults would walk by, smiling as they joyfully offered each of us handfuls of grains, a symbolic gesture that spoke of abundance and inclusion.

It wasn't just about survival; it was about solidarity—about ensuring that no one in the village was left behind. That celebration embodied the values that held the community together. *How can I serve the people in my life?* This question constantly echoed through my mind, especially during such ceremonies where the community's strength far outweighed that of the individual. *How can I be a light for other people to shine?* From my father, I learned that it was never about power but responsibility—about showing up for those around you and ensuring that everyone has their share of the harvest, both in grain and in opportunity.

He was the first person from his village to graduate from high school, a monumental achievement for someone from such humble beginnings. He later earned a *Doctorat d'État* and became a respected geographer and one of the most sought-after experts in the development field, especially in rural mountains. But despite his academic and professional successes, he remained humble, always grounded in the values of service and community. I remember watching him balance his national projects with helping neighbors or distant relatives. Whether offering advice, lending a hand, or simply being present, my father always made time for people. His humility extended beyond his actions—it was reflected in his deep appreciation for the oral culture of our community. He made it his mission to document and preserve the prose and poetry of local tribal artists from all walks of life, known or unknown, whether women or men. He kept an agenda filled with their verses, cherishing their stories and creativity. Through this, he cultivated a profound love for art and an attentive ear for those in the shadows, teaching me to value every voice, no matter how quietly it speaks.

There were countless evenings when people would come to our home in Rabat, sometimes unannounced, seeking my father's help. And he never turned them away. *What is the purpose in life if not service?* I would often ask myself as I observed him. He wasn't just solving problems—he was empowering others, ensuring they had what they needed to thrive. This was a pivotal moment for me, and it was the catalyst that propelled me to do the same. It was about making a positive impact on the lives of others. In his autobiography, my father reflected on the values he learned from my grandfather, emphasizing the essence of collective effort and service. He wrote: "The pinnacle of cooperation and mutual solidarity among people lies in each contributing what they possess and have to offer—from human resources, both men and women, to the strength of animals. May he rest in peace, my father consistently underscored the importance of artisans maintaining continuous humility, for they are always learning. Diligence and excellence are paramount, to avoid gaps that provide others the opportunity for criticism or disparagement."

These words encapsulate the ethos of a life lived with purpose, rooted in humility and a commitment to uplifting others. My grandfather, though never formally educated, held a deep understanding of the importance of learning and collaboration. For him, every person, every contribution, was vital to the survival and success of the community.

My father carried forward this legacy, embodying it in his work and daily interactions. His belief in humility and continuous learning didn't just apply to artisans; it became a guiding principle in his own life. Through his words and actions, he taught me that service is not an obligation—it's a privilege, a way to honor the connections we share with others. It is this perspective, my father's reflections remind me that the greatest impact we can make often lies in the smallest, most unassuming gestures, in the quiet acts of diligence and care that ripple through the lives of others.

My mother, Fanida Taha Ikli, had such a profound influence on my life, though her style was quieter and more behind the scenes. She didn't seek the spotlight, but her presence shaped everything around her. She created a home that radiated warmth. Hard work and empathy were not merely values; they were woven into daily life. She didn't have the opportunity to go to school when she was younger, but I remember her determination to learn. When I was a teenager in middle school, I would see her grabbing her books and heading to literacy classes every day, studying with the same dedication as any student a quarter her age. She never said much about it, but her actions spoke louder than any words could have. It was as if she were teaching me, without saying a thing, that it's never too late to grow, to learn, to strive for more.

Her quiet strength extended into every part of her life, even in the small things. One memory that still makes me smile is her love of baking. My mother made all sorts of cookies—different flavors, textures, and shapes. She'd store them in buckets, and while in many homes, buckets were used for water, in ours, they were reserved for these sweet treasures. I loved sneaking into the kitchen to eat as many as possible, sometimes grabbing one from each bucket just to sample them all. They were so delicious that it felt like a secret indulgence every time.

But one day, everything changed. We were hosting a big family party—maybe it was for my youngest sister's birth celebration—and my mom had prepared more cookies than ever. Since so many guests and people were coming in and out, she decided to store the buckets in my father's office, a safe place away from wandering hands. And then, she handed me the keys. It felt like she was handing me the keys to heaven, to those delicious cookies I loved so much. But this time, something shifted inside me. The moment she placed the keys in my hands, trusting me to guard her hard work, I couldn't bring myself to eat a single cookie.

For the first time, I wasn't the mischievous child sneaking treats in secret. Instead, I felt the weight of the responsibility she had placed on my shoulders. At that moment, I realized what trust meant. I realized that integrity isn't just about following the rules when someone is watching—it's about doing the right thing when no one is. That day, standing there with those keys in my hand, I learned a lesson I would carry with me for the rest of my life. My mother, without ever having to say a word, had instilled in me a sense of integrity that became my guiding compass.

What makes this memory even more powerful is that my mother didn't read about trust or leadership in a book. She didn't hear it on a podcast or attend a seminar. She lived it, day in and day out, through her actions. She valued autonomy and responsibility, not just for herself but for those around her. And she empowered me, not by micromanaging or hovering, but by trusting me to make my own choices.

That simple gesture—handing me the keys to the cookies—became so much more than just a responsibility for a party. It was her way of showing me that she believed in me, that she trusted me to be responsible, to hold myself to a standard of integrity. I owe much of who I am today to her quiet empowerment. She made me the man I am today, someone who values honesty, integrity, and trust above all else. And while she may not have spoken about leadership, she embodied it in every act of kindness, every decision to trust, and every moment of grace she showed me. My mother's quiet influence taught me that it's not always about grand gestures or loud proclamations. Her silent trust shaped my understanding of responsibility and integrity, but it also taught me something deeper—*leadership isn't always loud*. Sometimes, it's about being there for the people who need you, quietly offering support without seeking praise. My mother's strength lay in her ability to listen and to be present for others in a way that made them feel valued. You can lead by showing up for others and offering comfort, support, or guidance when needed.

Together, my parents cultivated a household built on generosity and solidarity. These weren't abstract values—they were the daily reality of our lives. My father would tell me stories about standing up for what was right, even when it wasn't the easiest or most accepted path. He believed everyone had a role to play in making the world better. It wasn't about being in the spotlight but doing what was needed when needed without expecting a reward.

As I grew older, these lessons stayed with me. The values they instilled in me shaped my leadership philosophy. Whether I was in school, working with civil society, or eventually taking on roles with the World Economic Forum, the core of my approach remained the same: leadership is about service. It's about lifting others, helping them realize their potential, and ensuring no one is left behind.

Long before I truly understood the concept of leadership, I was observing it in the most subtle ways right at home. My father was the quiet center of every family and community gathering. He never had to raise his voice or demand attention, yet people naturally gravitated toward him. Whether refilling someone's plate during a meal or stepping in to defuse a heated conversation, his style was always rooted in care and humility. I watched how people felt seen and heard, and how they leaned into his calm presence. He didn't lead with authority; he led with compassion.

It wasn't just at home that I saw this side of him. People would often travel from our original village of Amejgag, or even from the larger town of Kelaat M'gouna, to our house in Rabat without knowing him personally. They had only heard of his reputation, and they came hoping he could help them. And help them he did. Whether offering advice, assisting with paperwork, or connecting them to someone who could help, he always made time for them. What stood out to me wasn't just how he solved their problems but also how he made them feel. He treated their concerns as if they were his own, and in doing so, he gave people a sense of belonging, a sense that they weren't alone in facing their challenges.

One of my clearest memories is when tribal leaders from our village would come to Rabat, asking him to run for political office. They trusted him, believed in his integrity, and were confident he could be their voice in parliament. And yet, every single time, my father declined. His response was always the same: "I don't need to be in parliament to serve my people." He was convinced that accurate service didn't require titles or political power. His leadership was quiet, humble, and rooted in the belief that serving others was not about status but responsibility. He didn't need recognition or noise to make a difference.

Watching my father serve others, not for recognition but because it was simply the right thing to do, shaped my understanding of what leadership truly meant. It was about showing up for them and ensuring they felt supported, valued, and uplifted. I learned that the most influential leaders are the ones who lift others and work to ensure that everyone around them feels safe and heard.

This understanding of leadership, rooted in service, has been my guiding principle. Whether I was leading a university group or working with global leaders, the core of my approach has always been to lift others to create an environment where everyone feels they belong and has something to contribute. This lesson has shaped not only my leadership but also my sense of duty to my community.

Generosity, one of the core values my parents instilled in me, has become a central part of how I lead. But it goes beyond material generosity. It's about being generous with your time, attention, and presence. It's about offering your support to others in ways that often go unnoticed. Staying late to help someone with a project, listening when someone feels unheard, or simply being there when others need you—that's where authentic servant leadership happens. These small, quiet acts of service build trust, strengthen bonds, and create a sense of solidarity that cannot be shaken.

In addition to generosity, empathy forms the bedrock of my leadership philosophy. Empathy means immersing myself in their experiences, feeling their emotions, and seeing the world through their eyes. When people know you genuinely care, they bring their best selves forward. I've prioritized empathy in every community-building effort or leadership position I've held. I've made it a point to listen, to understand what drives each person, and to create environments where people feel safe and heard deeply.

One memory that stands out was during a regional SHAPE event of the Global Shapers Community, where tensions were running high between the hosting hub. Different voices clashed, and it felt like no one was truly listening to one another. Sensing the growing frustration, I invited everyone into a room and ensured that each person had the opportunity to speak and share their thoughts.

People tend to jump in with a response, but I was clear from the start: everyone would have their turn to speak, and interruptions would not be tolerated. I emphasized that the goal was to listen, respect differing opinions, and acknowledge each perspective. As the conversations unfolded, the atmosphere began to shift. What initially felt like a room divided by opposing views transformed into a space of shared understanding.

The process wasn't quick—it took four hours—but it was worth every moment. Instead of defensiveness, there was empathy. Instead of division, we found common ground. I realized that most of the time, people simply want their concerns to be heard and acknowledged. Often, disagreements are less about genuine conflict and more about being lost in translation. By fostering an environment of respect and active listening, we were able to turn tension into collaboration and move forward as a unified group.

Empathy has been transformative in more than just community projects. I've witnessed how it can completely change the dynamic of a team. By listening deeply and being present for people, you can guide others toward shared goals and a collective sense of purpose. Every person on the team, regardless of their background or role, will feel valued. They'll come to know that their contributions matter, and because of that, they'll be more engaged, committed, and willing to go the extra mile. Empathy creates an inclusive atmosphere where everyone feels motivated to contribute, and that's where real progress happens.

This approach was especially crucial during one of the most challenging leadership moments I've faced: the crisis in Afghanistan. As the Taliban took control, the Global Shapers Community began receiving heartbreaking messages from members of the country. The situation was dire, lives were at risk, and our Afghan members were pleading for help. The messages were filled with fear and desperation, and I knew we needed to act quickly. But this wasn't something I could handle alone. It required the strength and unity of our entire global network.

The urgency of the situation was overwhelming. Every message painted a picture of chaos and danger, and the weight of responsibility was heavy. I vividly remember one message from an Afghan Shaper who expressed deep fear for their life and the lives of their family. It was a plea for help that cut through the noise, reminding me of the gravity of the situation.

Shapers worldwide reached out without waiting to be asked, offering their support. Some brought legal expertise to help navigate immigration processes, while others leveraged their government contacts to arrange evacuation flights. It wasn't about who held a specific title or role but the shared responsibility we all felt to protect our community members. Everyone understood that we had a duty to act, and that sense of collective responsibility fueled our efforts.

Here, I want to recognize Collin, Danielle, Dom, Kiran, Luigi, and Mary for their leadership, dedication, and commitment as the Global Shaper core team. Their relentless efforts in driving the rescue mission and the countless hours and days they spent supporting fellow Afghan Shapers were a testament to the true spirit of servant leadership.

One of the most striking examples of this collective action was when we were working to secure safe passage for some of our Afghan Shapers and their families. Every minute mattered, and the situation on the ground was constantly shifting. We faced countless obstacles, from securing flights to coordinating with embassies or governments. Shapers from different countries worked around the clock, communicating across time zones to get our friends to safety.

I remember the tension in the hours leading up to a critical moment. We had finally secured seats on a military flight, but the next challenge was getting our Shapers through the chaos into the Kabul airport, which was a military zone. Outside the airport was mayhem. There were thousands trying to flee and Taliban fighters lurking nearby. We made many calls to try to have some of our contacts connect with people on their end so our friends could get in. The night was long and nerve-wracking, but we all held our breath, hoping for good news.

Suddenly, and very late at night, word came through that there had been a deadly bomb blast outside the airport. It was devastating news. We didn't know if our friends and their families had made it through or if they had been caught in the explosion. The sense of helplessness in those moments was crushing. We had done everything we could, but it felt like the situation was spiraling out of control. All we could do was wait and hope.

Several hours later, a message came from the Shaper —the flight had landed safely in an Eastern European Country. Our friends and their families had made it. There was an overwhelming sense of relief, but it was bittersweet. The same gate that had allowed them to escape had been the site of tragedy for many others just a few minutes after. The reality of the situation weighed heavily on all of us. We had saved a few lives, but what about the others left behind?

This belief in collective responsibility was put to the ultimate test during the crisis. I received a call from a Shaper who, through an intermediary, had managed to secure an airplane to land in Afghanistan to evacuate the staff of his organization. There were extra seats available, and he offered them to us. While the price per seat was steep, what made the situation even more unsettling was the Taliban's demand: a separate "fee" to allow the plane to land, payable in COVID-19 vaccines. The ethical dilemma was gut-wrenching. Vaccines, a lifeline for so many, were being weaponized in a desperate bid for control.

I wrestled with the decision. It would have been easy to justify paying the fee—lives were at stake, and this might have been their only chance to escape. But I couldn't bring myself to engage in what was essentially corruption. I refused even to bring the request to my superiors, let alone attempt to source the vaccines at a time when global superpowers were competing fiercely for every single dose. The weight of that choice was heavy, knowing it meant that some might not make it out. Even now, I question whether I made the right decision.

Yet, in that moment, I chose to prioritize integrity—not just for myself, but for the organization and what it stood for. Leadership isn't just about solving immediate problems; it's about holding firm to your values when they're tested the most. Sometimes, the hardest decisions are the ones that feel like sacrifices in the short term, but they preserve the principles that guide us in the long run.

This experience cemented my belief in the power of collective responsibility. It wasn't just about providing practical solutions—it was about standing in solidarity with our Afghan members, showing them they weren't alone in their darkest hour. The strength of our global community, united by empathy and shared purpose, was a beacon of hope in an otherwise bleak situation. Leadership, in that moment, was about empowering others, about coming together as a community to face an impossible challenge and make a difference.

Personal experience plays a critical role in community building. Growing up in Morocco, with its vibrant mix of cultures, landscapes, and histories, shaped how I see the world. It was about understanding that every person's story matters. Every person's experience brings something unique to the community. My journey—navigating the challenges of international leadership and working within global organizations—has given me a unique perspective on the challenges and opportunities of building communities.

A deep belief in the power of collective action keeps me engaged with my local and global community. Over the years, I've seen how communities can create incredible change when united by a common purpose. I've watched young leaders from the Global Shapers take center stage at global forums like Davos, where their ideas and energy shifted conversations in powerful ways. These moments remind me why staying connected to and investing in our communities is essential. The impact we can make together is far more significant than anything we could achieve alone.

This belief in the power of community isn't just theoretical for me—it's deeply personal. I've been fortunate to have mentors and leaders who supported me throughout my journey. They guided me when I needed direction, challenged me when I doubted myself, and celebrated my successes. That's why I feel a responsibility to pay it forward. As others empowered me to find my voice, I'm committed to empowering the next generation of leaders to create lasting change in their communities.

In my many encounters with Global Shapers and Young Global Leaders, we always discussed the next generation's challenges, from climate change to inequality, from education to the role of artificial intelligence; we always had something everyone is passionate about contributing to through insights but also projects. The room is always filled with ideas. But what struck me most wasn't the solutions we were proposing—it was the sense of shared responsibility. Everyone in these rooms understood that the problems we face as a global community can't be solved alone by one person or group. It will take all of us working together to create the kind of world we want to live in.

This sense of collective responsibility drives me. Whether working with a local community group in Morocco or collaborating with global leaders, I always seek ways to unite people. From the most miniature village in Morocco to the grandest stages of the World Economic Forum, the lessons I learned from my family and my personal experiences continue to guide me.

Like many other stories from my leadership journey, the Global Shapers' story during the Afghanistan crisis has reinforced this truth. It's not about me. It's about the people I'm privileged to work with and the communities we serve together. Every life we touch and every person we support is a testament to the power of collective responsibility and empathy. And as long as we continue to lead with those values, we cannot limit what we can do.

CHAPTER 3: **NURTURING LEADERSHIP**

"I am because we are, and since we are, therefore I am."
– African Proverb

The first time I set foot on the campus of Al Akhawayn University in Ifrane was during a trip organized by my father's university, Mohamed V University of Rabat, for the families of its staff. I was in middle school, and my father registered me with my cousin, Hamadi, who was living with us at that time and pursuing his bachelor's degree in physics and chemistry. Nestled in Ifrane, at an altitude of 1665 meters above sea level and known to locals as the "Little Switzerland" for its Alpine-style architecture and stunning natural beauty, the university felt like something out of a dream. As we drove through the main gate, I was in awe. The sloping red-tiled roofs of the buildings and the green landscapes framed by snow-capped mountains looked otherworldly. The crisp, cool air differed from anything I'd experienced before. The campus had a calm, almost magical feel, and for a brief moment, I imagined myself walking around as a student.

But that daydream quickly vanished when I learned about the tuition fees. They were exorbitant, around $11,000 per year, far beyond what my family could afford. I remember standing there, feeling a little deflated, thinking, *this place is for the elite, not for someone like me*. I brushed the idea aside. Al Akhawayn University wasn't a place for a boy from a modest family like mine, or so I thought.

One evening, a few years later, my father approached me with an application form for the university. "*Tawakal ala Allah* (Rely on God)", he said, "don't disqualify yourself. Let others disqualify you." He handed me the form with a look that left no room for argument. His faith in me was unwavering, and I knew what to do. So, I filled out the application. I didn't have high hopes, especially since the university uses English as a first language, and I didn't speak a word of it, but I followed his advice. Weeks later, after being invited for an interview and the general admission test, an unimaginable thing happened: I was accepted. Not only that, but I was also awarded a scholarship and a student loan that would cover 90% of my expenses.

I felt a mix of emotions—pride, disbelief, and excitement. The dream that once seemed out of reach was now a reality. I, a boy like me, would study at Al Akhawayn University alongside students considered part of Morocco's elite. My father's belief in me had opened a door I never thought I would walk through, and I knew I had to make the most of it.

The journey to the university was a significant one for me. It was the middle of August 2000, and like every summer, we were in the south at my family's home in Kelaat M'gouna. My father drove me to Tinghir, 70 km away, where I boarded the intercity bus to Azrou, a city 19 km away from Ifrane. It was a long, quiet ride that took the whole night, but I felt a sense of independence for the first time. Before I left, my father gave me—for the first time—some pocket money—1,000 dirhams, around $110. As I clutched the bills, I realized this was more than money. It was a sign that I needed to handle this new chapter independently.

The town was still asleep when the intercity bus pulled into Azrou in the early morning hours. I waited at a small café, sipping tea and trying to calm the nerves building up. As I stared at my reflection in the window, I decided to trim my teenager mustache in the café's restroom—a small act, but it felt like a rite of passage into adulthood. This was my first step into a world I had never known, and I wanted to enter it ready.

When I arrived at the university, I was struck by the beautiful campus's appearance in the early morning light. The towering trees cast long shadows over the manicured lawns, and the buildings looked majestic, just as I had remembered from my first visit. I saw families arriving with their children, helping them settle in. I was alone, but I felt a sense of pride. I had made this journey alone, and now it was up to me to prove I belonged here.

Orientation was overwhelming, but one thing stood out to me immediately—the student activities. I had never heard of this concept before. The idea that students could participate in activities beyond academics, that there were clubs and organizations to join, and that university life could be so vibrant, fascinated me. A whole new world was opening before me, and I was determined to explore it all.

Al Akhawayn University in Ifrane quickly became more than just a place for academic learning. It was where I discovered who I was and what I was capable of. I joined several student organizations, eager to get involved and make the most of my time there. One of my first roles was president of the Explorers Club. It was my introduction to leadership, and I quickly realized that leading my peers required new skills. Each student came from a different background, and I had to learn how to communicate effectively with each of them.

I was elected president of the Explorers' Club after I helped the Student Activities Office organize the "Trip to The South", one of the most memorable moments in my student life. During my first trip with the Explorer's Club, and since my father educated me very well about the region, I was proclaimed the touristic guide of the group. I took the initiative to invite my university friends to my family's home in Kelaat M'gouna. For some, it would have seemed like a simple visit, but for me, it meant much more. Growing up, I heard whispers and judgments about where I came from but never allowed that to affect my feelings. I was proud of my roots, and I wanted to share that with my friends. I didn't care if they would judge me for our modest home or my family's way of life. What mattered was that I shared with them a piece of my heart, offering them a glimpse into my world. When I called my late uncle to inform him that I had brought 50 students, his reaction was perfect. In our local Amazigh, he said, "*Mrahba ghissoun*," which means "You are all more than welcome."

Those words, "You are all more than welcome," stayed with me long after that day. They were a powerful reminder of the values my family had instilled in me—the significance of sharing, of opening our world to others without hesitation. This wasn't something I came to understand by myself. It became a lesson inspired by my father, who could regularly bring his college students home at some stage in their field journeys. The numbers never mattered to him, whether ten people or twenty. What truly counted was bringing people together, providing what we had, and doing so with an open heart. It was never about seeking approval or recognition. It was about service and giving selflessly, without any expected return. This lesson has stayed with me my entire life, shaping how I strive to lead.

I discovered this even more deeply that day as I sat on the carpet sprawled in our living room, sharing tea with my college friends. In that moment of connection, of being together without barriers, I noticed the power of community. It wasn't about someone's status; it was about how we came together, shared stories, and created something bigger than ourselves. After the trip and the moments of connection, many friends encouraged me to take on a leadership role. They asked me to run for president of the Explorers' Club. Though I had never sought a leadership position, I knew this was where my journey into navigating leadership began. It doesn't start with ambition or titles; it starts with service. It's about showing up as your complete self, offering what you have, and inspiring others to do the same. I learned that leadership isn't about status—it's about walking beside people, creating a path where everyone shines.

It wasn't easy initially, but I quickly learned that listening was the key. People wanted to feel heard and understood; everything else fell into place once you started listening. We organized trips, events, and activities, and each time, I felt myself growing more comfortable in my role.

One of the most defining moments at Al Akhawayn University in Ifrane was being elected president of the Student Government Association (SGA). The responsibility felt heavy on my shoulders, but it was also a challenge I was eager to take on. Suddenly, I wasn't just representing a small club but the entire student body. People came to me with their concerns, ideas, and frustrations, and I knew I had to be the one to advocate for them.

The role taught me invaluable lessons about accountability. In a leadership position, people entrust you with their concerns, and it becomes your responsibility to deliver results. We spent countless late nights drafting proposals, organizing meetings, and negotiating with the university administration. One particularly memorable instance of advocacy on behalf of the student body was our campaign to improve the quality of food services on campus.

The issue was clear: the meals the contracted restaurant company provided were of poor quality, and students had enough. Determined to demand change, we voiced our concerns strongly and threatened to walk out of the university restaurant altogether if action wasn't taken. This collective resolve sent a powerful message to the administration, showing that students were serious about holding the institution accountable. Our determination paid off. Not only was the contract with the current vendor terminated, but we also secured a seat at the table during the selection process for the new provider. It was a hard-fought victory that demonstrated advocacy's power and persistence's importance.

One of the most challenging aspects of leading the SGA was attending all disciplinary councils and defending the students. Sometimes, cases were easy, like plagiarism, but others were hard to handle. Sometimes, we had to find common ground with the administration and create a sense of unity. It wasn't always easy, but I learned that open communication was the key.

My involvement in founding the AUI-TV, the university's media organization, was another turning point. I had no prior experience in media, but I was drawn to telling stories and creating something that would engage the entire student body. Working with a small, passionate team, we produced parody comedy video clips highlighting essential campus events and providing a creative outlet for everyone involved. Live debates with the president and the administration leadership were something new on campus, and through this, students had access for the first time to a lot of information. I saw the power of media in connecting the stakeholders and fostering a sense of community.

Stepping outside my comfort zone was one of the biggest challenges I faced. As an introvert, being at ease around large groups or meeting new people didn't come naturally to me. The thought of navigating social dynamics often felt overwhelming. However, stepping into leadership positions forced me to confront these limitations head-on, pushing me to develop skills I didn't think I was capable of. Over time, I realized I didn't have to abandon my introverted nature; instead, I needed to learn to balance it with the demands of leadership. This balancing act led me to discover my ambivert nature—the ability to adapt fluidly between introverted and extroverted tendencies depending on the situation. I came to understand that embracing both sides not only strengthened my leadership skills but also allowed me to connect more authentically with others.

Over time, I found ways to manage my introverted tendencies while striving to be an effective leader. I discovered that introversion could be a strength, offering focus, reflection, and the ability to connect deeply. I also learned that many of the world's most inspiring speakers are introverts—they continuously refine their style, leveraging their introspective nature to craft meaningful messages. This helped reframe the way I viewed this particular trait of mine, allowing me to view it in a positive light.

For me, it became a matter of preparation, mindfulness, and deliberate practice. I focused on the task at hand, paid close attention to my thoughts, and centered myself through controlled breathing to calm my nerves. Over time, I developed techniques that became almost second nature. Visualizing success before stepping into a room, practicing measured gestures, and controlling the rhythm of my speech became tools I could rely on. Once deliberate and effortful, these techniques eventually turned into automatisms—patterns my mind and body adopted naturally whenever I found myself in these leadership positions. That being said, this transformation didn't happen overnight. It required consistent effort, a willingness to reflect, and a determination to improve with each experience. Even now, there are moments when I find it difficult to approach unfamiliar people or make cold calls—whether to book a restaurant or handle an inquiry. I often prefer using digital tools or automated systems to avoid direct interaction. While these tendencies remain a part of who I am, I see them not as limitations but as areas of growth. Leadership is an ongoing journey, and like many aspects of it, this is still a work in progress. What matters most is the commitment to keep trying, to adapt, and to grow with every experience.

I can say that being an active student was definitely the key for me to unlock this aspect. I immersed myself in various clubs and leadership roles, becoming known as one of the most active students on campus, and even being recognized for this during the end-of-academic semesters' celebration. Eventually, the university introduced a rule limiting students to holding executive positions in only two clubs at a time. I had been president of the Explorer's Club, Tamesmount Nel Akhawayn, AUI-

TV, the Student Government Association, vice president of the Diplomacy Club, and an executive member of AUI Radio. The list went on, but I stopped counting after a while.

Despite my successes, there were moments when I doubted myself. I struggled with impostor syndrome, the persistent feeling that I didn't deserve to be in the rooms I found myself in. Even though I was taking on leadership roles and receiving recognition, a part of me always wondered, *Am I perfect enough?* I feared that one day, people would realize I wasn't as capable as they thought. This feeling haunted me, especially during high-profile moments when I was expected to represent the university.

One of those moments came when I was asked to greet President John Agyekum Kufuor of Ghana during his visit to Al Akhawayn University in 2003. On the surface, it was an incredible honor. But internally, I was filled with anxiety. *Why me?* I kept asking myself. Why had they chosen me to meet a president out of a thousand students? I felt like an impostor, terrified that people would see through the façade that had become my very being and realize I didn't belong there.

Amid my self-doubt, a professor pulled me aside and gave me advice I've never forgotten. "He's just human," the professor said, smiling. "At the end of the day, he uses the toilet like the rest of us." It may have been a crude statement, but it was exactly what I needed to hear. It unlocked me! At that moment, the fear and anxiety that had been building up inside me dissipated. I realized we are all human, no matter how powerful someone seems. We all have our vulnerabilities and our doubts.

Meeting President John Agyekum Kufuor was an incredible experience, not because of the prestige but because I could approach him as another human being. That lesson stayed with me throughout my journey. I learned that it's not about pretending to be perfect or flawless. It's about showing up as your authentic self, even when uncertain or afraid. The moments of doubt I experienced reminded me that it is about being genuine and that vulnerability can be a strength.

Thanks to experiences like meeting President John Agyekum Kufuor, I was deeply immersed in the world of global affairs and diplomacy. This exposure was further enriched by my academic journey, where I pursued a double major in International Cooperation and Development and North Africa Studies, along with a minor in Women and Development. Adding to this was the invaluable opportunity to interact with students from diverse international backgrounds, broadening my perspective even further. The campus was a melting pot of viewpoints, and every conversation or event was an opportunity to see the world through a different lens. I attended conferences, engaged in thought-provoking discussions, and helped organize impactful events like the United Nations Pan-African Youth Summit in 2004. These experiences were not just academic exercises; they were windows into the complex world of international cooperation and diplomacy, helping me grasp the world and its multiple facets.

The lessons I absorbed at Al Akhawayn University in Ifrane, rooted in concepts like impostor syndrome, authentic servant leadership, and many others, would later become central to my work with international leaders and changemakers. The university instilled a deep belief that authentic leadership goes hand in hand with service. This idea—that leadership is not about power but about lifting others and creating a lasting impact—became a guiding principle for me. I saw firsthand how leaders who focus on service rather than power are the ones who inspire real change. Al Akhawayn taught me that leadership is about serving the greater good, and that lesson has been the foundation of my journey ever since.

CHAPTER 4:
YOUTHFUL LEADERSHIP

"The best way to find yourself is to lose yourself in the service of others."
– Mahatma Gandhi

One of the most defining experiences in my early leadership journey occurred in 2008 when I participated in the Euro-Med Youth Parliament in Alexandria, Egypt, and later in Berlin, Germany. These were not just my first visits to these incredible cities; they were also my first real introduction to international youth leadership. The excitement I felt walking into those rooms, surrounded by passionate young leaders across the Mediterranean, was electric. Each person brought unique perspectives, ideas, and a shared desire to create meaningful change. In these settings, I began to grasp the power of collective action and the potential for youth from different countries to unite around common goals.

The energy in those rooms was palpable, leaving a lasting impression on me. I recall moments when conversations flowed so easily between us despite our diverse backgrounds because we all had one thing in common: the desire to make a difference. It was here that the seed for my future work in international cooperation was planted.

Thanks to my participation in the Euro-Med Youth Parliament, I was later selected to attend the first Arab Youth Forum in Ain Soukhna, Egypt. At this forum, the idea for a Consultative

Youth Committee for the League of Arab States was born. As I sat with other youth leaders, brainstorming ways to amplify the voices of young people in the Arab world, I felt we were on the brink of something historic. It was a moment of pride but also a profound sense of responsibility. This initiative could potentially shape the future of youth participation in the region.

However, the opening plenary of the summit was a stark contrast to our vibrant vision for the forum. To our dismay, the stage was dominated by speakers who were all above sixty and male—"old dudes", as some jokingly referred to them—who lectured us at length about youth. Ironically, they were far removed from the realities of the younger generation they were addressing. It felt like a forum *about* youth rather than a forum *for* youth.

During our daily debrief as organizing committee members, my friend, Sarah Zaaimi, and I raised a pivotal question: "Is this truly a youth forum, or just a forum about youth?" We argued that if it was the former, young people should speak, facilitate, and take center stage. The person in charge, Dr. Khalid Louhichi, the visionary Director of Population Policies and Migration at the League of Arab States, listened to us with an open mind. Bit by bit, he embraced the idea of giving youth a platform and agreed to let us moderate the next panels.

We approached this opportunity not as a revolution, but as an evolution. To ensure meaningful participation, we established clear speaking rules, limiting each speaker to no more than a set number of minutes (I believe it was seven). This structure allowed as many young voices as possible to engage actively in this groundbreaking youth forum. By making these changes, we set a precedent for future forums under the League of Arab States—a space where youth actively led the conversation. Unfortunately, this vibrant dynamic stopped after Dr. Khalid Louhichi retired from the League of Arab States.

Shortly after, I was selected to serve on the committee, an immense honor that would eventually lead me to one of the most life-changing experiences of my journey: attending a training for youth leaders on intercultural dialogue in Budapest, Hungary in April 2009. It was my first time in Hungary, and I remember the excitement as I wandered through the streets of Budapest, marvelling at the mix of history and beauty around me. The city blended old-world charm and modern vibrancy, and I felt a deep connection to its atmosphere.

But what truly made that experience unforgettable wasn't just the training itself—it was the moment I met my future wife, Marie.

It was a warm, sunny day, and after a long journey of travel, I found myself sitting in the garden of the European Youth Centre in Budapest, taking in the peaceful surroundings. As I sat there, trying to unwind, she walked over. She was young and intelligent and had this spark in her eyes that drew me in. Her blonde hair caught the sunlight, and there was something effortless in how she carried herself. She was from Switzerland and had a natural elegance shaped by her involvement in international affairs and the Swiss Network for Models of the United Nations.

We started talking casually about our shared passion for diplomacy and youth leadership and soon found ourselves deep in conversation about international affairs and youth empowerment. Something about her sharp intellect and warmth left me speechless. I could feel an instant connection that went far beyond the professional collaboration we were embarking on. There was something extraordinary about her, and I knew that this moment might forever change my life.

Throughout the training, we worked closely together, preparing for the upcoming Euro-Arab Youth Conference in Assilah, Morocco, where we co-facilitated sessions on intercultural dialogue and migration. It was an incredible experience knowing that what started as a professional collaboration would soon grow into something much more profound. I still remember the excitement of working alongside her, the late nights of preparation, and the spontaneous laughter that would erupt when we were too tired to think straight. Every moment we spent together felt significant, as though our paths had crossed for a reason.

One of my fondest memories from the Budapest training wasn't just the sessions themselves but the adventure we embarked on afterwards. It was a Saturday evening, and we had just finished the day's work. Instead of eating dinner and then returning to our accommodations, a few of us—broke but adventurous youth leaders—decided to hop on a train to Vienna, Austria. We hadn't planned it; it was a spur-of-the-moment decision, and we embraced it with the excitement only youth can bring.

After grabbing a midnight dinner at a fast-food restaurant in Vienna, we found ourselves at a nightclub, the only open place where we could pass the time since we had yet to book a hotel. The night was filled with laughter, music, and dancing. We were the only ones in the club that night. I'll never forget the fun we had as we took turns on the dance floor, ensuring the place stayed lively and open until it was time to leave.

At around 5:00 AM, some of our friends had to return to catch their flights back from Budapest, but four of us, including Marie, looked at the big screen of departing trains and decided to hop on another one, but this time to Bratislava, Slovakia. Why not! We arrived early on a quiet Sunday morning, and the city felt almost deserted. The streets were empty, and most places were closed, but we found a small café that welcomed us, offering hot chocolate and croissants. We sat there, warming ourselves with the drinks and enjoying the peacefulness of exploring a new place.

There was a sense of adventure as we wandered through the quiet streets. Everything seemed so serene, almost like the city was our own to discover. We walked with no particular destination in mind, soaking in the beauty of Bratislava and enjoying each other's company. There was no rush, no need for an agenda—we were living in the moment, savoring the spontaneous adventure. In those hours, it became clear that this wasn't just an ordinary trip. It was one of those rare experiences where everything seemed to align, and our connection grew more assertive.

The adventure ended as we returned to Budapest for our flights, but that day stayed with me. It wasn't just about traveling to different cities or experiencing new places—it was about bonds, friendships, and the realization that life's most memorable moments often come from the unplanned and unexpected: the best plan is no plan!

That realization carried over into my work with diverse youth groups, where the bonds we formed were often tested by the challenges of bringing together people from different cultural backgrounds, experiences, and expectations. While those challenges were real—marked by language barriers, differing values, and unique communication styles—they also became opportunities for growth and connection. I quickly learned that empathy and patience were critical to overcoming these obstacles. By listening and understanding each person's perspective, we could find common ground and work together toward shared goals. Diversity, which initially seemed challenging, soon became one of our greatest strengths.

As I continued my journey in youth leadership, I realized more than ever how essential youth inclusion is for driving global change. Young people, after all, are the ones who will live with the consequences of the decisions made today. Their involvement in shaping those decisions is not just significant—it's crucial. Youth bring fresh perspectives, bold ideas, and a willingness to challenge the status quo. Their creativity and passion have the power to disrupt traditional systems and drive innovation in ways that more established leadership often cannot.

My early involvement in regional diplomacy occurred during the Euro-Arab Youth Conference in Tunisia and Italy in 2010. The conference brought together young leaders from across the Arab and European regions, and it was one of the most interesting experiences of youth activism on difficult topics such as migration and cultural dialogue. It began in Tunisia, where participants engaged in workshops that explored the various dimensions of migration, including its economic, social, and humanitarian aspects. But what made this experience truly unique and impactful was the journey that followed. The participants boarded a ferry, tracing the same route countless migrants take when risking their lives to reach Europe. It wasn't just a symbolic act—it was meant to help the young leaders understand the gravity of the issue on a profoundly personal level.

As the ferry sailed across the Mediterranean, the conversations among the participants grew more serious and reflective. This wasn't just about theoretical debates or policy discussions anymore. The journey gave them a glimpse into the reality that migrants face, creating a lasting sense of empathy. The group dynamic had shifted when they arrived in Sicily, Italy. The young leaders were no longer simply discussing migration from a detached, academic perspective—they were approaching it with a renewed sense of purpose and responsibility.

In Sicily, the discussions continued, now enriched by the shared experience of the ferry journey. The young leaders came together not to impose their ideas or engage in divisive debates but to listen, collaborate, and build solutions. It was incredible to witness how the shared experience of walking in the footsteps of migrants had transformed the group. They were no longer just representatives of their countries—they were young people united by a common cause, working together to solve a complex global issue.

As a facilitator, my role was to guide the discussions and help the participants connect on a human level once they reached Sicily, Italy. I watched as they found common ground, not through argument or competition but through empathy and understanding. This was a powerful reminder of the potential of youth-driven diplomacy. This experience solidified my belief in the importance of empathy in leadership. Diplomacy isn't just about negotiation or persuasion—it's about creating shared experiences that foster understanding. It's about recognizing each other's humanity and using that understanding to bridge divides.

The ferry journey and the time spent with these leaders taught me that the most influential leaders could listen, see beyond their own experiences, and find common ground with people from different backgrounds. I would carry this lesson with me for the rest of my leadership journey: empathy is the bridge that connects people and creates lasting solutions.

I continued to be engaged in youth diplomacy, always considering the lessons I had learned in those early years. Youth inclusion, cross-cultural dialogue, empathy, and listening became the cornerstones of my approach. I knew that if we wanted to create meaningful change in the world, we needed to give young people a seat at the table and ensure their voices were heard. It wasn't just about having a place in the room but empowering them to actively shape the conversations and solutions.

My commitment to advocating for youth inclusion has always stemmed from my belief that young people are an essential part of the solution to the world's challenges. It's not just a matter of representation. Youth make up 50% of the global population and bring unique insights, bold ideas, and a willingness to challenge outdated systems. More importantly, they will live with the outcomes of today's decisions, so it only makes sense that they have a say in shaping those decisions.

Throughout my journey, I've seen how young people can drive innovation in ways established leadership often cannot. They approach problems with fresh perspectives, unburdened by the constraints of tradition. Their passion and energy can disrupt stagnant systems and push us toward more sustainable and inclusive solutions. This is why youth inclusion is not just important but essential for creating a better future.

My experiences in various youth leadership forums, such as the Euro-Med Youth Parliament, the Consultative Youth Committee of the League of Arab States, and other youth diplomacy conferences, have shaped my professional approach to leadership. These forums were transformative, showing me firsthand the power of diverse perspectives and the impact of collaborative leadership.

CHAPTER 5:
GLOBAL LEADERSHIP

"Act as if what you do makes a difference. It does."
– William James

My journey to the World Economic Forum (WEF) wasn't straightforward. It was a culmination of years spent dedicated to youth activism and the deep desire to make an impact far beyond my local community. From a young age, I felt a calling to not just participate in society but to lead in a way that could drive meaningful change. My passion for diplomacy and international cooperation was ignited while I immersed myself in global affairs at Al Akhawayn University in Ifrane. Yet, the road to WEF had many twists and turns, with uncertain moments shaping my resolve and commitment to the causes I cared about.

After earning my master's degree in Euro-Mediterranean Affairs, which took me through Italy, Spain, and Morocco, I completed an internship at the European Institute of the Mediterranean in Barcelona, Spain. When I returned to Morocco, I dreamed of entering the diplomatic world and joining the Ministry of Foreign Affairs. This had been my goal forever, a career path I had envisioned for myself. But as I soon learned, reality has a way of throwing unexpected obstacles.

Despite me going through the interview and being told that I'd be joining the Ministry, I couldn't assume a position due to bureaucratic inefficiencies. I was told that I needed an equivalency for my diploma—a document certifying the recognition of my foreign degree, which I earned at the University of Granada in Spain. I went through the exhausting and costly process of translating my master's degree documents (syllabus, internship report, admission papers...). Then, I was asked for a certificate from the Spanish government recognizing my master's degree, which was issued by the University of Granada, a Spanish public university. With the certificate in hand delivered by the Embassy of Spain in Morocco, I was left waiting with no response. It was disheartening. I had left my previous job at Toyota for this new endeavor, and Marie, my future wife, had moved to Morocco, ready to start this new chapter with me. But instead of a new beginning, I found myself without a job and a clear path forward. It was a period filled with deep frustration and even depression.

But life has a way of redirecting us when we least expect it. Amid this uncertainty, I took on a role at the Rabat School of Governance and Economics as the Deputy Director of Student Affairs. The school was launched a few months earlier as Morocco's first political science school. It was exciting work, but deep down, I felt pulled toward something more significant—international relations and cooperation. My passion for diplomacy and international affairs and the desire to contribute to global efforts kept tugging at me. It felt like I was meant for more, but I didn't know how to get there, so I started by organizing events and conferences with the diplomatic circles in Rabat and the Moroccan political parties.

Then, in September 2011, an unexpected opportunity came my way. A friend from the Euro-Mediterranean Youth Parliament, Melih Tara, then Senior Manager Global Shapers Community at the World Economic Forum, contacted me with the opportunity to launch the first Global Shapers Hub in Morocco. This was a chance to mobilize young leaders and connect them to a global platform. I didn't hesitate for a second. I accepted, and that's how my journey with the World Economic Forum began.

The Rabat Hub quickly grew into something impactful. After several months of leading it, the WEF team approached me with a more significant opportunity: managing the Global Shapers Community across the Middle East and Africa. Initially, I hesitated. Marie is Swiss, and the idea of moving to Switzerland, especially as someone from the Global South, was daunting—would people think I had married her to move north? Our relationship was built on love and respect, and I didn't want that to be questioned.

In the end, a pivotal conversation changed my mind. At the first Annual Curators Meeting in Geneva in August 2012 hosted at the World Economic Forum, I spoke with my friend Melih while hiking in the mountains surrounding Zermatt in the Swiss Alps. He encouraged me to stop worrying about what others might think. "Your career and personal life are yours—not someone else's—to judge," he told me. His words resonated with me. Why was I letting the opinions of others dictate my decisions? It was time to take control of my path and assume responsibility. With a renewed mindset, I applied for the role.

When everything seemed to fall into place with the first interviews being successful, life threw another curveball. In December 2012, I was invited to Geneva for the final round of interviews for the WEF position. I had my visa appointment, but there was a last-minute delay, and I got the visa only 20 minutes before my flight. I missed the flight. I decided to drive to the Casablanca airport, the biggest in Morocco. Marie and a travel agent were checking for any flight going to Europe that evening. There were no other flights that day from any Moroccan airport to Europe; all were full. I had to accept that this opportunity might slip through my fingers. It felt like the door had closed shut before giving me a chance to peak behind it. But sometimes, setbacks are just pauses, not endings.

I was invited to the World Economic Forum on Africa in Cape Town five months later. I spoke in one of the official sessions, supported other Shapers throughout the event, and stayed highly engaged during the meeting. What I hadn't realized was that the Global Shapers team present at the event had taken notice and were impressed. One day after the Forum meeting ended, I was contacted by Yemi Babington-Ashaye, the head of the Global Shapers team, asking if I had a visa to Switzerland, which was the case. I was invited to another round of interviews in Geneva. This time, everything aligned perfectly. I was offered the position, and it felt like a culmination of all the hard work, perseverance, and passion I had put into my journey.

The transition to Geneva, often seen as the epicenter of global diplomacy and governance, wasn't just a career move for me—it was fulfilling a lifelong passion. Here, I truly began to understand the importance of operating at the intersection of international organizations, NGOs, and governance structures. The World Economic Forum gave me the platform I had always dreamed of—a space where youth leadership, diplomacy, and global impact could converge. The Forum allowed me to elevate the voices of young people from underrepresented regions to ensure that their ideas were part of international decision-making. I was honored to have my work recognized in 2020 when I was selected among the "*Quinze moins de 40 ans qui font la Genève internationale.*" This prestigious recognition highlighted the "fifteen individuals under 40 that are shaping the International Geneva," underscoring my role as part of "*the vanguard of global governance*." This acknowledgement was not just a personal milestone but a validation of the years of dedication to fostering youth engagement, intercultural dialogue, and collective action on a global scale. Being selected among this group of leaders, who were described as the "pioneers of tomorrow's global governance," reaffirmed my belief in the power of youth-led initiatives to shape the future. I connected local youth movements from Mogadishu, Amsterdam, Recife, to Irvine, and Erbil through WEF with global decision-makers. I witnessed the power of giving young people a seat at the table—how their ideas and perspectives could shape decisions directly affecting their lives. The fulfilment I gained from this work was immense. It wasn't just about creating opportunities for youth to speak; it was about ensuring they had real influence.

Leading the Global Shapers Community and the Young Global Leaders (YGLs) programs at WEF has been one of my most significant career experiences. The Global Shapers Community is built on the idea of local action with global impact. It empowers young people in cities worldwide to take ownership of the challenges in their communities and become problem-solvers and catalysts for change. My role allowed me to see the tremendous potential of youth at the local level—people who may not have traditional leadership roles but are driving change in their ways.

Global Shapers initiated projects that addressed critical issues like climate change, inequality, education, and mental health. It was humbling to witness how these local initiatives could inspire broader movements and influence policy when amplified on a global stage. Their work's impact was a testament to the power of grassroots leadership, which emerges from within communities, driven by shared experiences and collective action. It reinforced my belief that authentic leadership doesn't always come from traditional hierarchies.

The Young Global Leaders (YGLs) program represented individuals already recognized for their leadership on a global scale—people who were influencing industries, governments, and organizations worldwide. Leading the YGL Community was about engaging with leaders who were already driving large-scale impact but seeking ways to collaborate and deepen their influence and leadership. It was about bringing together some of the brightest minds to solve the world's most challenging problems.

In the YGLs program, I saw how leadership at the highest levels could be enhanced through collaboration across different sectors, cultures, and geographies. The diversity of ideas and the genuine willingness to work together for the greater good were inspiring. Our role as a team was to create an ecosystem where these two forms of leadership—local and global—could thrive. We made a more significant collective impact by leveraging each other's strengths.

One of the most defining moments in the Global Shapers Community's growth and success came during the COVID-19 pandemic. The pandemic created a sense of urgency, and the Shapers were quick to act. The COVID-19 Recovery Report testified to the community's adaptability in uncertain times. Hubs worldwide worked tirelessly to provide personal protective equipment (PPE), support local healthcare systems, and create mental health support networks for their communities. Thousands of young leaders stepped up when governments and traditional systems struggled to meet the demands of the crisis. Their actions during this time proved that youth leadership is not just about planning for the future but responding to the present challenges.

Over a decade, the community grew from a small initiative to a global force, driving thousands of projects impacting millions of lives. From climate action to education initiatives, the community showcased how young people can transform grassroots movements into lasting solutions when given the right platform. We scaled up the community's activities significantly, launching innovative projects that crossed sectors, cultures, and regions.

One key milestone in our efforts was a partnership with the former US Vice President Al Gore and his Climate Reality Leadership Training. We had almost no projects addressing the climate crisis at that time. However, after having hundreds of Shapers participating in Al Gore's climate training, the focus of the community shifted dramatically. Within a few years, we went from having no climate-related projects to running over two hundred projects annually. This transformation was a great achievement for the whole community, as it demonstrated how young leaders could be mobilized to tackle one of the most pressing challenges of our time.

Another major collaboration that had a significant impact was our partnership with Accenture, which focused on fostering responsible leadership among young people. Through this collaboration, we launched initiatives that helped young Shapers develop the skills to lead ethically, sustainably, and with a deep commitment to social responsibility. Hundreds of young leaders worldwide benefited from this partnership, gaining the tools they needed to lead successful projects and do so in a way that prioritized long-term impact and accountability.

In January 2019, six Global Shapers were named co-chairs of the World Economic Forum's Annual Meeting in Davos. This decision marked a significant turning point for youth leadership on the global stage. The Shapers were no longer just participants in global discussions—they were now leading them at the highest level. This moment symbolized how deeply embedded the voices of young leaders had become in shaping international policy. Watching them stand before heads of state, ministers, and CEOs, not only speaking truth to power but challenging the very foundations of those in the room, was deeply humbling. Among them was Mohammed, a refugee who had spent over 20 years in a refugee camp, his entire world confined to those boundaries. Seeing him on that global stage was a moment I will never forget. His presence wasn't just powerful—it was transformative.

I still hear Mohammed's words echo in my mind, especially when he posed the question that silenced the room: "My story is inspiring, and I get that. But what do I inspire you to do?" His voice carried the weight of decades of suffering, resilience, and hope. His story, shared with unwavering courage, laid bare the stark contrast between the lofty ideals discussed in Davos and the harsh realities of human suffering. He spoke of ethical and sustainable development, of humanity's aspirations to solve complex issues like artificial intelligence, and even the pursuit to "solve death." But then, with heartbreaking simplicity, he asked, "And yet, there is so much human suffering... We haven't even figured out life yet."

The journey to bring Mohammed to that moment was not one that I or anyone else could have done alone—it was a team effort and a culmination of years of work and dedication. It took courage, determination, and countless conversations to bring voices like his into the spaces where they matter most. It's never easy to bring diversity to the table, especially in such elite environments, and convincing others of the value of doing so is even harder. But this is where we need to truly show up as leaders—by pushing against the grain, by believing in the importance of representation, and by creating the conditions where unheard voices can be elevated.

Securing travel documents for Mohammed, someone who had never held a passport or even an identity card, was just the beginning. Preparing him for the overwhelming cultural differences he would face in Switzerland—his first time flying, his first time using a keycard to open a hotel room, his first time stepping beyond the refugee camp—was a monumental task. We worked together as a team to ensure he had the support and coaching to share his story in a way that could resonate in such a formal, global setting.

These firsts for Mohammed, which so many of us take for granted, were not just logistical hurdles—they reflected the courage it takes to bring someone like him to a space like Davos. It wasn't easy, and it wasn't without its challenges, but it was absolutely worth it. Mohammed's presence on that stage was about the power of inclusion, of showing the world that voices like his are integral to shaping our future.

Bringing such voices forward is often the culmination of years of work and effort. It requires resilience and a deep belief in the power of diversity to create meaningful change. It's not easy, and sometimes it's a struggle to convince others of why it's necessary. But when it happens, as it did with Mohammed in

Davos, it becomes clear that those moments are what leadership is all about. It's about building the bridge between different worlds, creating a platform where all voices, no matter how marginalized, can be heard and can shape the conversation.

Following moments like Mohammed's at Davos, where the power of collective voices was brought to the global stage, I'm reminded that this strength is not limited to formal settings like the World Economic Forum. This collective power—this constellation of human potential—exists in every facet of life. From our families to our professional teams to our circles of friends, leadership is not about elevating a few stars but about creating a star team. It's about connecting individual talents, so they complement and elevate one another, making something greater than the sum of its parts.

The Global Shapers Community became a powerful example of what youth leadership can achieve with the right platforms and resources. By giving these young leaders a seat at the table in major WEF meetings, including the prestigious Annual Meeting in Davos, we amplified their voices on a global stage. Every year, we prioritized ensuring that the Shapers had opportunities to engage with global decision-makers—not just as passive participants but as integral contributors to the agenda. Their local experiences and stories were essential in shaping discussions about the future of governance, climate, technology, and social justice.

The experience of leading the Global Shapers and witnessing this transformation in youth leadership influenced my understanding of leadership. My time at the WEF solidified a broader philosophy: leadership is not about power or control but about collaboration and bringing diverse perspectives together to tackle complex global issues. The WEF provided a unique platform where leaders from all sectors—heads of state, CEOs, civil society leaders, and young change-makers—came together to address the world's biggest challenges. It taught me that authentic leadership requires building bridges between stakeholders and facilitating collective action for the common good.

Apart from leading these two communities, one of the most transformative experiences within the WEF was my participation in the Global Leadership Fellowship Program (GLFP). This program, which I joined as part of the 2013-2016 cohort, was a three-year journey designed to develop leaders equipped to address global challenges. The GLFP wasn't just about academic learning; it combined experiential leadership with personal development, pushing fellows to redefine how they viewed leadership in a world increasingly requiring systems thinking and cross-sector collaboration.

One critical framework that we embraced during the GLFP was systems thinking. With all the challenges that lie ahead of us nowadays, solving problems in isolation isn't possible. It's about understanding the interconnected nature of global issues and leveraging insights from multiple disciplines to create sustainable solutions. This approach taught us the importance of seeing the bigger picture, recognizing and identifying when different systems influence one another, and making sure to collect the dots before connecting them.

The program emphasized the importance of emotional intelligence and self-awareness. Through personal assessments, emotional intelligence tests, and leadership inventories, we gained valuable insights into our strengths and areas for growth. The program's focus on self-reflection helped me understand our impact on those around us. It was crucial at this stage to acknowledge that it's about knowing ourselves before leading others, being aware of the limitations and constantly striving to improve the self. Coaching and peer review sessions gave us a deeper understanding of how our leadership style could evolve.

During the program, we participated in an extraordinary retreat in Gemmi, nestled in the breathtaking Swiss Alps. This mountain retreat was an intense, purpose-driven experience designed to challenge us beyond our limits. It pushed us out of our comfort zones, compelling us to function as a cohesive team in an environment that demanded resilience, adaptability, and trust. We were tasked with leading and collaborating under pressure, navigating real-time challenges that tested our ability to communicate effectively and build trust amidst uncertainty.

One unforgettable night stands out vividly in my memory. Around 11 p.m., the group was divided into smaller teams, each given an assignment with a deadline looming early the next morning. What we didn't know at the time was that some of these groups were handed assignments deliberately designed to disrupt the work of others. Their task? To subtly influence or convince the other groups to alter their efforts—all without revealing their true objective. It was a masterclass in leading without authority, persuading without concrete evidence, and collaborating while exhausted.

By 1 a.m., the cracks began to show. Tensions ran high as the strain of fatigue and the ambiguity of the exercise pushed us to our breaking points. For some, the process felt authoritarian; for others, it seemed absurd—a deliberate masquerade orchestrated to frustrate and confuse. Yet, beneath the surface, it was a meticulously crafted trust stress test. Could we navigate the chaos, maintain composure, and collaborate despite conflicting objectives and fraying nerves?

The experience was elevated by the guidance of two world-renowned experts: Gianpiero Petriglieri from INSEAD and Daniel Shapiro from Harvard University's Conflict Resolution Program. Their insights and dedication transformed what could have been a simple exercise into a life-changing lesson. They pushed us to reflect deeply on the dynamics of trust, leadership without formal power, conflict resolution, and the importance of clear communication under pressure.

Looking back, I am grateful for the experience. It acted as a mirror reflecting our strengths, weaknesses, and potential as leaders. The lessons in resilience, teamwork, and the power of shared leadership that emerged from that retreat continue to shape how I approach challenges to this day. It wasn't just about surviving the night; it was about learning to thrive in the complexities of leadership and human connection.

Another session that has profoundly shaped my understanding of leadership occurred during a module at the London Business School, where we had the chance to engage with exceptional leaders, including the former Head of British Police, or as they are named, the Scotland Yard. His insights on decision-making in times of ambiguity and crisis resonated with me deeply, reflecting the complexities of leading in today's world. However, a simple question he asked left the most significant impact on me: "How many of you want to be remembered after you pass away?" Without hesitation, almost everyone in the room raised their hands.

He followed up with a second question: "How many of you know the names of your great-great-grandparents?" The room fell silent. No one raised their hand. He smiled and said, "These are your family members; you don't even know their names. And yet, you think your great-great-grandchildren—or the world—will remember you?" It was a humbling moment that reminded me of the impermanence of personal legacies. Leadership, he implied, isn't about seeking to be remembered by the world—it's about making a difference in the lives of those around you, here and now.

The diversity of my cohort in the GLFP was another critical factor in shaping my leadership philosophy. My peers came from over 20 countries, bringing their unique cultural and professional backgrounds to the program. This diversity enriched every discussion and project, reinforcing the importance of inclusivity in leadership. Whether we were tackling sustainability challenges, exploring design thinking, or discussing the US public health, the range of perspectives in the room added depth to our problem-solving efforts.

The GLFP also stood out for its practical application of leadership. It wasn't just about theoretical learning; we were given opportunities to put our skills into practice by working directly with world leaders, CEOs, and global decision-makers. Events like the WEF Annual Meeting in Davos provided the perfect stage to practice what we had learned in real-world settings. These experiences allowed us to bridge the gap between leadership theory and practice, learning firsthand how to navigate complex stakeholder dynamics and make decisions in high-pressure situations.

PART 2:

SERVANT LEADERSHIP AND COMMUNITY INNOVATION

CHAPTER 6:
THE POWER OF "WE"

"A leader is best when people barely know he exists."
– Lao Tzu

By now, I think you know that authentic leadership for me is not about commanding from the front. It's about creating a space where others can step up, share their ideas, and take the lead, whether in a community setting or elsewhere. This approach, rooted in servant leadership, emphasizes empathy, service, and empowering others. Like a museum curator carefully selects and arranges different kinds of artworks to create a meaningful experience, a community leader must recognize each member's unique strengths, ensuring everyone's voice and competency are valued.

I love how in the Global Shapers Community, the hub leaders are called "Curators." This title is more than a name; it reflects how the community would like the hub leaders to approach leadership. Like a leader, a curator doesn't overshadow the art but highlights each piece's beauty. Similarly, a Curator in the community works to ensure that every member's strengths and experience are acknowledged, creating a place where everyone fits in and feels at home. It's about building a space where every individual's contribution is celebrated, just like each piece of art in a gallery.

The community is like a gallery filled with diverse talents and perspectives. The Curator's role is to create an environment that respects each member's uniqueness while blending their contributions into a powerful collective effort. It's about setting up a flexible, transparent structure that allows everyone to participate in the process. For me, a true leader is someone who doesn't just manage people but helps them grow. Leadership means prioritizing the well-being and growth of others and guiding them to reach their full potential.

Decentralized leadership models, like those used in the Global Shapers Community, make this growth possible. Instead of keeping all decisions at the top, responsibility is shared across the community. This approach allows new leaders to emerge and gives everyone a sense of ownership. It's like allowing each member to add their piece to the community's story. This way, leadership becomes a shared journey, with everyone contributing to the path forward.

Leadership is about understanding people's actual needs, not just what they ask for. It requires a deep sense of character—knowing what's right and standing by it, even when it's tough. As James Hunter said, "Leadership is simply a character in action." It's about having the strength to do what's suitable for those you lead, even when it's not an easy choice. Leadership means care: being kind, humble, putting others first, and trusting them honestly.

In the Global Shapers Community, the Curator should not wield power over others. Instead, they build trust and encourage teamwork. They guide others with humility, listen carefully, and provide growth opportunities. By fostering an environment of trust, the community, through its governance, inspires others to step into leadership roles, creating a space where everyone is encouraged to be their best.

I have often described our world as a VUCA environment—a space defined by volatility, uncertainty, complexity, and ambiguity. This framework captures the relentless pace of change and the unpredictability that leaders must navigate. In such a world, adaptability and resilience are not just valuable; they are essential. Leaders must respond to shifting realities with clarity of vision and decisiveness, all while maintaining a sense of direction amidst the chaos.

However, Paolo Gallo, in his insightful book, *The Seven Games of Leadership,* introduces a provocative evolution of this concept. He suggests that we are transitioning from VUCA to what he calls "WTF moments"—an era where "What The F***" becomes a fitting description of the unprecedented disruptions and absurdities that define our time. Citing *1000 WTF Moments* by Jim Slatton, Gallo argues that these moments demand not just adaptability but deep reflection, as the old playbooks no longer apply, and patterns seem to dissolve entirely.

This shift highlights a profound difference in the challenges leaders face today. With VUCA, leaders contended with ambiguity and uncertainty, but there was still an underlying structure to lean on, however unstable. In contrast, WTF moments present situations so unexpected and irrational that they often defy comprehension, let alone traditional responses. Leaders must develop a new level of emotional intelligence, creativity, and resilience to navigate this environment. They need to embrace uncertainty as a factor and a constant.

The contrast between these two paradigms is illustrated below:

Feature	VUCA (Volatile, Uncertain, Complex, Ambiguous)	WTF Moments (What The F***)
Nature of Challenges	Predictable in unpredictability; patterns exist but are unclear	Unpredictable and often nonsensical; patterns seem to disappear
Leadership Approach	Adaptive, resilient, and visionary	Deeply reflective, emotionally intelligent, contextual intelligence and innovative
Core Skill	Navigating complexity with agility	Embracing chaos and leveraging emotional and relational strength
Goal	Maintain clarity and direction despite the fog	Find meaning and purpose amidst disorder
Example	Responding to economic downturns with strategic foresight	Grappling with sudden, irrational global disruptions like COVID-19 or geopolitical shocks

The transition from VUCA to WTF moments underscores an urgent call for leaders to rethink their strategies and mindsets. This isn't just about handling disruption; it's about redefining leadership for a world where the unexpected is the norm. Leaders must not only be comfortable with chaos but must also inspire others to find strength and meaning within it. Sure, the journey from VUCA to WTF is a shift in terminology, but more importantly, it is a fundamental reimagining of what it means to lead in our time. Thus, servant leadership means more than just responding to challenges. It's about anticipating what's next (the unknown unknown) and building resilience in our systems. By encouraging continuous learning and adaptation, leaders can prepare their communities for whatever comes their way. During uncertain times, this type of leadership helps create stability. It's about looking ahead, ensuring the community is ready for change, and working together to create lasting solutions.

I often emphasize the importance of character and doing what's right, even when no one is watching. It is about guiding others with honesty and integrity, setting the example for others to follow. The real test of a leader comes when no one is observing; it's about how consistently we adhere to our values, especially when there's no recognition or reward. The number of exceptions we make toward our values should be close to zero. This unwavering commitment to principles is what builds trust and shapes the moral compass of the leader.

Hunter's book, *The Servant*, offers valuable lessons on leadership. He explains the difference between power and authority. Power means making people do things, even if they don't want to. Authority, however, is about leading through respect and trust. It's about inspiring others to follow because they believe in you, not because they have to. This distinction is crucial, especially when working with volunteers who are part of the community because they care, not because they are paid. A leader cannot rely on power in a volunteer community like the Global Shapers, where people participate out of passion. No paycheck or contract binds them. Instead, leadership builds trust and earns respect through consistent actions and service. People follow because they believe in the mission and the leader, not because they must.

Leadership and management are often referred to interchangeably; however, they serve different roles. Peter Drucker once said, “Management is doing things right; leadership is doing the right things.” Management oversees projects, ensures tasks are completed efficiently, and hits targets. It’s all about operations and making sure things run smoothly. Conversely, leadership is about setting a vision and inspiring people to reach their full potential. It’s not just about getting tasks done; it’s about helping people grow and believe in a bigger goal. I once heard someone say leadership is management without ambiguity. Somehow, these roles are complementary, each fulfilling a critical need within an organization. Managers excel at ensuring things get done; they bring structure, process, and accountability to the table. However, they often miss the leadership component—the part that focuses on caring for and empowering the people they oversee. On the other hand, leaders can sometimes remain anchored in vision-setting and the philosophy of care without translating these ideals into actionable results. Both approaches are essential, particularly in the business world, where a contract between employer and employee goes beyond mere task completion. A true symbiosis between leadership and management creates an environment where people feel both inspired and supported, where big ideas are not only envisioned but also realized through effective execution. When these models work together in harmony, they drive productivity and a culture of mutual respect and shared purpose.

During my time with the Global Shapers Community and the Forum of Young Global Leaders, I saw firsthand how significant this difference is. A leader’s job is not to micromanage every detail but to create an environment where people can succeed. It’s about providing the resources, trust, and freedom they need. While a manager might focus on deadlines and deliverables, a leader prioritizes their team members' development, ensuring their growth aligns with the community's vision.

I remember a conversation with a team member struggling with a new responsibility. She came to me, clearly stressed, saying, "I'm afraid I'm not doing this right. Maybe I'm not cut out for this." I had watched her work closely over the past months, and I knew without a doubt that she had the skills and potential to excel. Her dedication, attention to detail, and ability to learn quickly had already impressed me on multiple occasions. I listened carefully and replied, "You're doing better than you think. Mistakes are part of the process. Let's work on this together, but remember, I trust you to figure it out." Her expression softened, and I saw a new determination in her eyes. It wasn't about taking over the task for her but showing that I believed in her ability to succeed and reminding her of the qualities that had already proven she was more than capable. Sometimes, all someone needs is a little extra reassurance and a reminder of their own strengths to move forward with confidence.

This belief in people is at the heart of my leadership philosophy. I've always felt that when you trust people, they rise to meet the challenge. Micromanaging does the opposite—it makes people doubt themselves and stifles their creativity. Leaders who focus on control limit their teams' potential, while those who trust and empower unlock incredible results. When people feel trusted, they become more confident, take ownership of their roles, and deliver their best work.

In his book *Leaders Eat Last*, Simon Sinek discusses creating a "Circle of Safety" where people feel secure and valued. This concept resonates with me. As a leader, I see it as my duty to create this circle for my team. It's about ensuring that they know I'll stand by them even when things go wrong. I often told my team that I'd take a bullet for them, and that's exactly what they expect from me. At the same time, they know precisely what

I expect from them. This mutual trust creates an environment where they feel secure enough to take risks, push boundaries, and innovate without the fear of failure or reprimand.

When I joined the World Economic Forum, a friend asked me about the biggest difference between working in Morocco and at the Forum or Switzerland in general. My immediate response was trust and care. In Morocco, as much as I love my country, there is an unfortunate reality: you often spend a significant portion of your career working to earn the system's trust. It's a continuous process of proving yourself over and over again. However, it felt remarkably different at the Forum and in Switzerland in general. There, they trust you from day one, until you give them a reason not to.

In my first week, I experienced this difference firsthand. I was handed a Forum Gold Credit Card and told, "Just take a picture of the receipt when you buy something." There were no extensive forms, no bureaucratic delays—just immediate trust. I was also given a phone with international roaming and the ability to make calls anywhere in the world. The message was clear: They believed in my competence and integrity from the outset, and this trust wasn't something I had to battle for.

The same sense of trust struck me when I had my first visit to the doctor in Switzerland. After the appointment, I walked to the reception, fully prepared to settle the bill. To my surprise, the receptionist simply smiled and said, "No need to pay now; we'll send you the bill." I was taken aback. I went home and told my spouse, who is Swiss and familiar with the system. I asked her why they didn't request payment upfront.

"Did you give them your insurance card?" she asked.

"No," I replied, "I forgot it."

"Did you give them your address?"

"Yes," I said, pausing to reflect. That's when she added, with a knowing smile, "You're thinking like a Moroccan now. You're wondering if someone could give a fake address and avoid paying the bill."

She was right. I considered it, even for a fleeting moment. In Morocco, I grew up in a generation where "being smart" often meant finding ways to outwit the system. It was almost a cultural reflex. People would brag about not paying taxes, skipping queues, or using their connections to evade responsibilities. These acts were seen as clever, even admirable. But beneath that surface, such behaviors erode trust—the glue that holds communities together.

In Switzerland, trust is not just a value; it's a cornerstone of society. Everyone is expected to honor their responsibilities, and this mutual respect creates a system that functions with remarkable efficiency. Reflecting on this experience, I couldn't help but mourn the gradual fading of this value in my country, Morocco. Trust was once central to our communities, a vital force that kept people connected and cooperative. But over time, it has been overshadowed by a culture that often rewards opportunism over integrity. Trust isn't just a social nicety—it's a fundamental building block for any thriving society. Without it, systems falter, relationships break down, and the collective good is sacrificed for short-term individual gain—a powerful reminder of what communities lose when trust is no longer cherished or upheld. Trust became the foundation of my approach to leadership. But it's not just blind trust—it's trust backed by consistent support and accountability. I believe in giving my team the space to make decisions, knowing I'll be there if things don't go as planned. If they succeed, the credit is all theirs; if they stumble, I'm there to help them. This approach fosters a culture where everyone feels they can contribute without fear of being blamed if things go wrong.

However, trust alone isn't enough. Leaders also need vision. John P. Kotter, in *Leading Change*, highlights the importance of having a clear vision that inspires and guides the team. Managers might focus on short-term goals and daily tasks, but leaders must consider the team's long-term goals. They must paint a picture of success and engage others in bringing that vision to life.

One of the most fulfilling parts of leadership is seeing people grow—both in their roles and as individuals. A leader's vision must include not only the organization's goals but also each team member's growth. It's about challenging them to step out of their comfort zones and supporting them as they learn and improve. Vision isn't just about looking to the future; it's about ensuring the team has the right tools and support to get there.

Trust is a cornerstone or even pre-requisite of any thriving community and leadership. Aside from being a nice-to-have quality, it's essential for building a safe space where people feel free to share, collaborate, and innovate. Trust makes people feel comfortable expressing their ideas without fear of judgment. It is the invisible thread that binds individuals to each other and the mission they are working toward. Without trust, even the best ideas struggle to gain momentum because the foundation for teamwork is missing.

So, leadership isn't just about making decisions; it's about doing so in a way that reflects the organization's values. Transparency and consistency are key. When people know they can count on their leaders to be honest and dependable, they feel more secure and engaged in the work, and are intrinsically motivated to mirror this behavior. This sense of security allows a community to thrive even when facing challenges.

Servant leadership plays a central role in building this kind of trust. It's a leadership style that focuses on serving others first rather than seeking control. A servant leader listens, supports, and puts the needs of their team ahead of their own. This approach is critical in volunteer-driven communities, where people participate because they care about the mission, not because they have to. In this environment, authority doesn't come from a title but from earning respect and trust.

I often told my team, "My role is to clear the path for you and provide you with the necessary tools. You tell me, with your expertise, which steps we need to take." It's about being a guide, not a director. By giving people the freedom to lead in their own way, they often surprise you with their creativity and dedication. Trusting others to take the lead not only empowers them but also allows them to grow into their full potential. It shows that you believe in their abilities, and that trust fosters an environment where they feel confident to innovate and push boundaries.

This approach to leadership also aligns closely with Simon Sinek's teachings about creating a "Circle of Safety"—a concept we briefly discussed earlier. It's about ensuring people feel safe enough to take risks and innovate. In such an environment, trust flourishes, and people can do their best work. When trust is present, a community is resilient. It can face challenges head-on, knowing that each member is committed to supporting one another. It also strengthens relationships and fosters a sense of ownership among community members. When people feel trusted, they take pride in their work and are more committed to the community's success. They feel a deeper connection to the community's vision and are willing to go the extra mile to see it succeed. This kind of engagement transforms a group of individuals into a cohesive team.

In addition to trust, a robust set of ethical values is crucial for sustaining a healthy community. Ethics guide how decisions are made and how people interact with one another. Ethics provide the moral compass by which decisions are made, conflicts are navigated, and trust is built. In communities, values such as inclusivity, transparency, and accountability are at the core of everything, from decision-making processes to the way leadership is exercised. Ethics and values provide a shared language and understanding, guiding both leaders and members in how to interact with one another, how to align their personal goals with the collective mission, and how to handle conflict when it arises.

Ethics are not abstract ideals but living principles that govern the way the community operates day to day. As I'll share in the next chapters, transparency, for instance, is critical for building and maintaining trust in communities. When decisions are made openly and communicated clearly, members are more likely to engage fully, contributing their best efforts with the confidence that they are part of an honest and accountable community. Accountability, in turn, ensures that leaders and members alike are responsible for their actions, fostering a culture where integrity is valued and upheld.

CHAPTER 7:
LEADING WITH HEART

"Leadership is not about being in charge. It is about taking care of those in your charge."
Simon Sinek

Emotional intelligence is the foundation of the servant leadership style I thrive on pursuing. It's not something anyone can learn overnight, but a skill we must hone through experience, patience, and self-awareness. Emotional intelligence allows us to see beyond the words people say to understand what they truly feel and why they act the way they do. It's the difference between reacting impulsively and responding thoughtfully in a way that fosters trust and growth.

In his book, *Emotional Intelligence*, Daniel Goleman describes four key components of effective emotional intelligence: 1) self-awareness, 2) self-management, 3) social awareness, and 4) relationship management. Self-awareness involves recognizing and understanding one's own emotions, while self-management enables one to regulate the responses and maintain composure, even under pressure. Social awareness, which includes empathy, helps us attune to the emotions and perspectives of those around us, allowing us to see their struggles, motivations, and needs more clearly. Relationship management, in turn, equips us to build and sustain positive relationships, using empathy and insight to guide interactions toward constructive outcomes.

By developing these four components, we can remain calm under pressure, manage our own emotional triggers, and understand others' emotions not as obstacles but as pathways to stronger connections. Emotional intelligence becomes a powerful tool for building, allowing us to navigate challenging situations with clarity and compassion. Ultimately, emotions can divide us or bring us closer together, and how we handle them determines our paths.

In leadership, the real power of emotional intelligence comes into play when navigating challenges or conflicts. Rather than rushing to conclusions or decisions, it's crucial to prioritize assessing the emotional landscape. What are people feeling? What's driving their concerns—fear, frustration, or excitement? Understanding these nuances leads to better, more productive conversations.

I remember a particular instance that tested my emotional intelligence during a pivotal event in my leadership journey. In 2015, I was asked to lead the Annual Curators Meeting for the Global Shapers Community. The stakes were high, tensions were rising, and expectations from everyone involved were immense. However, what made the task even more challenging was the differing opinions of three highly influential figures—the Head of the Community, our Managing Director, and the Founder and Chairman of the World Economic Forum, Professor Klaus Schwab.

Each had a vision of how the opening plenary should unfold. The Head of the Community emphasized one message, the Managing Director another, and the Founder had a different focus. At first, I felt like I was being pulled in every direction. Every conversation added a new layer of complexity. But instead of letting frustration get the best of me, I had to find a solution, so I began by listening, not just to their words, but to the emotions behind their messages. I realized their goals weren't as contradictory as they seemed. The friction was caused by their differing communication styles, not their underlying intentions.

They were all passionate about the same core message but expressed it differently.

So, I reframed the situation. Instead of seeing their input as conflicting, I treated it as complementary. I decided to approach each meeting with tailored communication. For every discussion we had about the opening plenary session, which was the focus of the tensions, I prepared three versions of the script, each reflecting the language and tone that resonated with them individually. The core message stayed the same, but the words were adjusted to fit their style. When the time came to sit down with all three, I handed them a program tailored to their perspective. Each leader saw their vision reflected in the document. I gave a general description, not going into details of that particular plenary and jumped directly to ask them about their preferences on another session where I knew they'd agree with each other. It was not about choosing one perspective over another, but rather giving them what they wanted to hear and see.

That moment taught me a valuable lesson. It's not about getting everyone to agree on every detail but about making people feel heard and respected. When you take the time to understand someone's emotional state, you can create solutions that satisfy everyone involved.

This approach has shaped the way I lead teams. Emotional intelligence helps me see that not everyone responds to challenges similarly. Some people need encouragement, while others need space. Some want clear action steps, while others prefer to process things independently. As a leader, it's my responsibility to recognize these differences and support people in the best way for them. It's not always easy or successful, but the intention is always there.

One of the outcomes of emotional intelligence in leadership is the trust it builds within a team. When people feel their emotions are acknowledged and respected, they are more likely to engage fully and contribute their best work. They become more resilient because they feel connected to something bigger than themselves. They're not just following orders; they're part of a community where their feelings matter.

Emotional intelligence also drives creativity and innovation. When people feel emotionally safe, they take risks, offer bold ideas, and aren't afraid of failure. They know their leader will support them, even if things are unplanned. This psychological safety is crucial in environments where creativity is vital. People can only think outside the box when they're not afraid of being judged or dismissed.

The ability to navigate emotions also extends to the broader community. As a leader, it's essential to recognize that not everyone faces the same struggles. Some may feel overwhelmed, others may feel marginalized, and others may thrive under pressure. Emotional intelligence allows us to create an environment where everyone feels supported and empowered, regardless of their emotional state.

Developing emotional intelligence in community leaders starts with leading by example. I always emphasized the importance of self-awareness, listening, and empathy in leadership. It wasn't enough to know these values in theory; we had to practice them in real-time, especially when things got tough. I encouraged other leaders to be mindful of their emotional reactions and to pay close attention to the feelings of those they led.

Leaders need to give others opportunities to practice and foster emotional intelligence. For instance, ask their team members or community members to take on roles where they have to mediate conflicts or handle difficult conversations. Sometimes, they'll have to support a struggling member or be on the seat firing someone they worked with. These situations aren't easy, but they require leaders to tune into the emotional needs of others, listen carefully, and respond with empathy. It is in these moments that their emotional intelligence would genuinely grow.

Empathy became a driving force in the Global Shapers Community. By taking the time to understand the group's diverse experiences and perspectives, we created initiatives that truly mattered. Empathy helped us see beyond words. It allowed us to hear the emotions behind the conversations and sense when someone was hurting or excited. It turned simple interactions into deep, meaningful connections. This openness is the foundation of strong community bonds.

The Global Shapers Community had its share of difficult moments, from internal conflicts to facing more significant global crises. But it was through emotional intelligence that we could navigate these moments effectively. Trust was key. People trusted each other because they knew their emotions would be valued just as much as their contributions. Focusing solely on tasks is easy, but the real challenge lies in ensuring that people feel heard, understood, and supported. It's not always about fixing the problem immediately. Sometimes, it was about validating someone's feelings, about saying, "I hear you or I see you."

Emotional intelligence allowed me to stay grounded in chaos and to help others feel more secure in uncertain times. Whether navigating conflict or brainstorming ideas, emotional intelligence made us stronger as a team. Emotional intelligence was not just a tool; it was the heart of our operation. It helped us build lasting relationships, foster collaboration, and achieve things that wouldn't have been possible without that deep emotional connection. Emotional intelligence gave us the power to navigate challenges with grace and to emerge stronger on the other side.

As we continue to grow, it's important to remember that it's not just about the work—it's about the people behind it. And when people feel seen, heard, and valued, there's no limit to what they can accomplish.

PART 2:

THE ART OF CURATING COMMUNITIES

CHAPTER 8: **CURATING A COMMUNITY: BALANCING ART AND SCIENCE**

"Vision without action is merely a dream. Action without vision just passes the time. Vision with action can change the world."
– Joel A. Barker

As a kid spending summers in Kelaa M'gouna, I used to sit beside my late grandma—and later, after she passed, my late Aunt Rkia—as they wove the traditional textile known as "Azta." I particularly loved when they created the recycled versions—taking old clothes, tearing them into strips, and weaving them into colorful carpets. These were sometimes placed under wool carpets to protect them from floor dust. Even though they were hidden, they were still beautiful. Every detail was remarkable and carried a story.

Building a strong and vibrant community, for me, is like putting together a puzzle. Each piece—whether purpose, identity, or emotion—fits together to create something meaningful and lasting. Every part needs to be placed with care and intention. Community building requires careful planning, attention to detail, and a clear understanding of how everything connects. A community's strength comes from how well these pieces come together, forming a foundation of unity, trust, and cooperation.

A community is a deliberately cultivated collective of people united by a shared purpose, values, and a profound sense of belonging. It is not static; rather, it is a dynamic, evolving entity where diverse voices are not only heard but empowered and engaged in collaborative action. The ultimate goal of a community is to achieve meaningful, lasting impact—something far greater than what could be achieved individually. A true community serves as a space where individuals are encouraged to grow, contribute to the common good, and together, forge a future that is inclusive, resilient, and sustainable.

In my journey, I've come to understand that community building is both an art and a science—a blend of emotional intelligence, strategic design, and deep empathy. The theory alone is not enough; it is through lived experience and active facilitation that communities are built, nurtured, and sustained. At its core, a community is where trust and collaboration are paramount and where the collective energy of the group drives change that benefits everyone involved.

Richard Millington's classification of communities into five types—Interest, Action, Place, Practice, and Circumstance—provides a valuable framework for understanding the diverse nature of communities and the specific leadership approaches each type requires:

- Interest Communities: These communities are driven by shared passions or hobbies. Leaders here must stimulate ongoing interest and create spaces where members can dive deeper into their passions. Such communities thrive on enthusiasm, and leaders must ensure discussions stay engaging and relevant.
- Action Communities: Focused on driving collective change, these communities require leaders who can inspire and mobilize members toward a common goal. Leadership in action communities is about sustaining momentum and ral-

lying people around causes they believe in, transforming intention into impactful action.

- Place Communities: United by geography, these communities benefit from leaders who are deeply connected to the local context. Effective leaders in place-based communities can navigate the unique challenges and opportunities specific to the area, fostering a sense of local pride and mutual support.
- Practice Communities: These are professional or skill-based communities where leaders must be subject-matter experts who can foster knowledge exchange and professional development. Leadership here is about creating an environment of shared learning, growth, and mutual support.
- Circumstance Communities: Formed in response to external events or shared experiences, these communities require leaders who are empathetic and skilled in navigating complex, emotional dynamics. The leader's role is to guide the community through its collective experience, building resilience and healing when necessary.

By recognizing these different types of communities, we gain insight into how leadership styles and strategies must be adapted to meet the specific needs of each community. A community, after all, is not defined solely by its purpose but by the emotional and social connections between its members.

Understanding the principles that underlie community building can help leaders create environments where trust, collaboration, and shared purpose thrive. There are several foundational theories that provide insights into how individuals connect, collaborate, and create meaningful impact together.

Developed by Robert Putnam, Social Capital Theory emphasizes the importance of networks, norms, and trust in the development of strong communities. Social capital is the connective tissue that holds communities together, facilitating cooperation, communication, and coordination among members. Communities with high levels of social capital are marked by increased civic engagement and a greater capacity for collective action. In my experience with both local and global communities, I've seen firsthand how social capital enables communities to thrive not just on shared goals but on the quality of relationships and the trust that exists among their members. Trust is a critical element, allowing members to feel safe, connected, and committed to the community's success. Without it, collaboration falters, and the community's resilience weakens.

Introduced by McMillan and Chavis, the Sense of Community Theory highlights four key elements: membership, influence, integration, and the fulfillment of needs, as well as a shared emotional connection. These elements are essential in fostering an environment where individuals feel they belong, believe they can make a difference, and find personal and collective value in their involvement. From my experience, this emotional bond—whether among Global Shapers or in the Forum of Young Global Leaders—is what sustains long-term engagement and fosters a collective identity. It's the glue that holds a community together, transcending geographic and cultural barriers. This theory provides the blueprint for how to create environments where members are connected and invested in the community's success, ensuring the community's longevity and strength.

The Collective Efficacy Theory proposed by Robert Sampson focuses on a community's ability to achieve shared goals through social cohesion and mutual trust. Communities with high collective efficacy are more effective at mobilizing resources, enforcing social norms, and addressing challenges collaboratively. This theory is particularly important in community building as it emphasizes the power of a shared belief in the community's capacity to achieve its desired outcomes. When members trust one another and believe in their collective ability to effect change, the community becomes more resilient and proactive in facing challenges, thereby enhancing its overall impact.

Community development is a multi-dimensional process that unfolds in distinct phases, each bringing unique challenges, opportunities, and lessons. Drawing from established community-building theories like Tuckman's (1965) group development model, Wenger's (1998) Communities of Practice, and McMillan & Chavis's (1986) Sense of Community, we can see that the journey of community building is not linear but cyclical, with each phase contributing to the long-term sustainability and impact of the community. This journey parallels my own experiences, whether in the Global Shapers Community or in personal milestones, where growth, collaboration, and reflection have shaped both individual and collective development.

1. **Formation: Establishing the Foundation**

The first phase of community development mirrors Tuckman's (1965) "Forming" stage, where individuals come together, united by shared goals or interests. This is the stage where the foundation of the community is established—its purpose, vision, and mission are defined. The focus is on building a collective identity and fostering a sense of belonging. McMillan & Chavis (1986) emphasize the importance of shared emotional connection and clearly define group boundaries during this stage. This is crucial for creating an environment where members feel safe to contribute and collaborate.

From my experience with the Global Shapers Community, this phase was about defining the community's ethos—establishing the core values that would guide its evolution. Just as I had to reconcile my own identity, growing up in Morocco and balancing my personal and cultural pride, this phase in community development requires careful alignment between individual identities and the collective purpose. In the Shapers Community, the mission to empower young leaders to drive positive change was co-created with the founding Curators, ensuring that everyone felt a sense of ownership and alignment with the community's vision.

The formation phase is a delicate balance of bringing together diverse perspectives while fostering a shared vision. This stage is crucial because it sets the tone for how the community will grow and evolve, much like the early stages of personal development, where the foundational values instilled in us shape our future decisions and behaviors.

2. **Involvement: Building Commitment and Engagement**

Once the foundational elements are in place, the next phase is Involvement, where members actively engage and begin to develop a shared identity and collective knowledge base. Wenger's (1998) Communities of Practice model is particularly relevant here, as it highlights how members begin to form a community of shared practice, co-creating knowledge and roles. This phase aligns with Tuckman's (1965) "Storming" stage, where initial friction may arise as members negotiate group dynamics, establish relationships, and define roles.

In this phase, individual commitment becomes critical. The community begins to establish its culture—how members interact, resolve conflicts, and contribute to the shared mission. Early relationships are built, and leadership roles start to take shape. Reflecting on my time as the Founding Curator of the Rabat Hub, I learned that this phase was about fostering trust and ensuring that everyone had a role to play. Much like my experiences in university, where I was entrusted to lead clubs and student organizations, involvement in community building requires leaders to empower others, ensuring that each member feels valued and has an opportunity to contribute.

In the Global Shapers Community, involvement came to life through shared projects, events, and initiatives. Hubs worked within local contexts to address challenges while simultaneously contributing to the global mission. This decentralized approach allowed for autonomy while maintaining a cohesive sense of purpose, demonstrating the balance between local action and global alignment.

3. **Growth: Expanding and Diversifying the Community**

As the community progresses, it enters the Growth phase, marked by expansion in both membership and activities. This correlates with Tuckman's (1965) "Norming" phase, where the community begins to establish its norms, and collaboration becomes more seamless and productive. Wenger's (1998) theory of Communities of Practice suggests that during this phase, the community's shared repertoire is enriched by new members who bring fresh perspectives and experiences.

In my experience with the Global Shapers, this growth phase involved rapid geographic expansion, with hubs being established in over 500 cities worldwide by 2022. The challenge during this phase is ensuring that as the community grows, it doesn't lose its core identity or mission. New members bring diversity, but they must also be integrated into the community's existing shared vision. This was particularly evident when we introduced Community Champions, a governance mechanism designed to support Curators and help manage the vast number of hubs. These champions played a crucial role in maintaining cohesion during periods of rapid growth, much like mentors and guides who help us navigate our personal growth journeys.

The Growth phase is also about deepening engagement. As communities expand, it is essential to ensure that members remain connected, not just to the mission but to each other. This requires intentional efforts to build relationships, foster collaboration, and ensure that the community's governance structures are flexible yet strong enough to support continued expansion.

4. **Maturity: Stability and High Functionality**

Once a community has expanded and established its norms, it reaches a phase of Maturity akin to Tuckman's (1965) "Performing" stage. At this point, the community stabilizes with clear leadership, well-defined norms, and structured activities. Collaboration becomes smooth, and the community operates at a high level of functionality. Members are not just participating; they are leading, innovating, and addressing more complex challenges as a cohesive unit.

In the Global Shapers Community, the maturity phase was marked by a shift from simply organizing projects to addressing deeper, systemic issues in local and global contexts. Hubs that reached this level of maturity began to focus on sustainability—ensuring that their initiatives had a long-lasting impact, and that leadership was continuously developed through mentorship and succession planning. Just as a personal journey requires ongoing reflection and adaptation, mature communities must continue to evolve while remaining true to their core values.

Maturity also brings the challenge of avoiding complacency. Just as in life, where moments of stability can lead to stagnation if we stop striving for growth, communities in the Maturity phase must remain vigilant, continuously seeking ways to innovate and improve.

5. **Sustainability or Evolution: Adapting or Transforming**

The final phase in the community development journey is Sustainability or Evolution. In this phase, communities either sustain themselves through adaptive strategies or evolve into new forms. Wenger's (1998) concept of Reification is key here, as abstract goals and values are translated into concrete actions, ensuring that the community's impact endures. Some communities may evolve to meet new challenges or transition to new structures, while others may decline as interests shift, reflecting Tuckman's (1965) "Adjourning" phase.

This phase is marked by the need for adaptive leadership. Communities must be agile, responding to external pressures and internal dynamics without losing sight of their mission. In the Global Shapers Community, this meant continually re-evaluating the governance structures, launching new initiatives, and ensuring that members remained engaged. This phase is about legacy-building—ensuring that the community's impact lasts long after individual members or leaders have moved on.

Sustainability also requires recognizing when it's time to evolve. Just as in personal development, where growth often requires letting go of old habits or beliefs, communities must be willing to adapt, transform, and sometimes even dissolve to make way for new opportunities.

Community development is not a linear journey but a cyclical one. Each phase builds upon the previous one, with moments of reflection and reinvention. Governance plays a critical role throughout this journey, providing the structure and support needed to guide the community through its phases of growth, maturity, and evolution. By embracing the lessons learned from each phase—whether establishing a strong foundation, fostering engagement, or adapting to new challenges—leaders can ensure that their communities remain vibrant, resilient, and capable of creating lasting impact.

One of the most essential elements in community building is shared purpose. This turns a group of individuals into a united team, all working toward a common goal. A shared purpose gives direction, helps people align their values, and encourages collaboration. But a few leaders cannot be solely responsible for deciding this purpose—everyone in the community has to have a hand in shaping it. This way, it becomes personal to everyone, something they feel connected to and motivated by.

The purpose of the Global Shapers Community was co-created involving all the different stakeholders. It wasn't just a mission statement handed down from leadership—it was a purpose shaped by everyone. This ensured that each person felt ownership of the community's goals. We first formed the Global Shapers' charter during the First Annual Curators Meeting in 2012 in Zermatt, Switzerland. I had the chance to attend it as the Founding Curator of the Rabat Hub. We debated and voted on each article of that charter. It was a long process, but it was worth it. Everyone involved felt like they were part of something much bigger than themselves.

This co-creation process didn't end after the charter was written. As the community grew, our purpose evolved to meet new challenges and opportunities. We didn't just stick with the same ideas forever. Each new generation of leaders brought fresh perspectives, and the purpose adapted with them. This adaptability allowed the community to stay relevant and robust, no matter how much the world changed.

Creating a shared purpose is just the beginning. To ensure that purpose leads to real action, we needed structure. This is where frameworks like the Vantage Points model help in the design process. MGTaylor developed this model, which helps align discussions and is essential in ensuring that everyone speaks the same language and has a unified understanding of the goals before moving forward with planning or execution. Losing focus or having conflicting priorities can be very easy without such a structured approach.

The Vantage Points model helps view every problem from different angles—like layers of nature, from the sky down to the soil. It starts with big-picture thinking and works to the most minor details, ensuring nothing is overlooked.

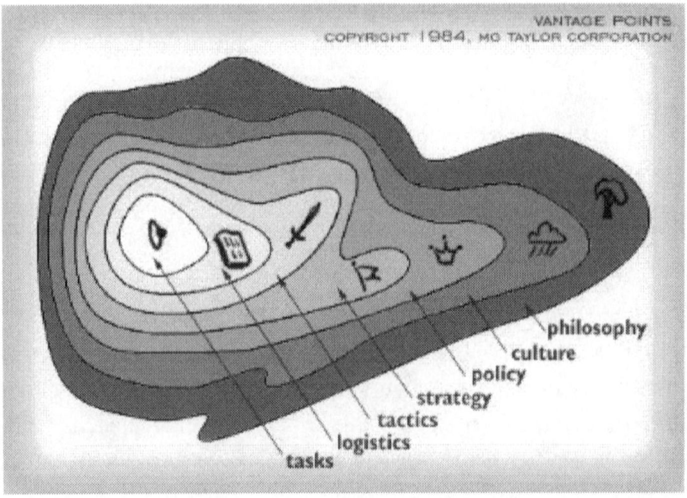

For example, we used the Vantage Points model to guide us when planning an event. In a meeting, we asked the big questions: "Why are we doing this? What impact do we want to have?" This was the philosophy level—getting everyone on the same page about the deeper purpose of the event.

Once we agreed on the philosophy, we moved to the next level, discussing culture and policy. How did we want participants to feel at the event? What kind of environment were we trying to create? We wanted everyone to feel included and heard, so we ensured our policies reflected those values.

After that, we got into the specifics of strategy and tactics. What sessions did we want to organize? Who would lead them? How would we ensure the event achieved its goals? This is where accurate planning begins—deciding how to turn big ideas into concrete action.

Finally, we focused on the practical details—logistics and tasks. Here, we ensured everything was in place to support the event, from booking venues to managing schedules. Each task was assigned to a specific person, and we ensured nothing slipped through the cracks.

Using the Vantage Points model allowed us to keep everyone aligned, from the high-level leaders to the grassroots participants. Whether we were planning a global summit or launching a local project, this model helped us structure our thinking and ensured that every decision was grounded in a shared understanding.

The Vantage Points model also helped us manage the complexity of working with diverse groups. Imagine being in a room where one person is discussing the big picture of climate change while another is discussing the details of planting a tree. Without a structured way to align these conversations, it's easy for discussions to become chaotic. The model gave us a way to organize these conversations, ensuring everyone was on the same page, even if they were tackling different parts of the project.

While shared purpose is the foundation of a community, the true strength of any group lies in the identity it builds among its members. As Daniel Shapiro, founder and director of the Harvard International Negotiation Program and YGL alum, often emphasizes, identity is the critical anchor that gives a community its sense of belonging, continuity, and direction. Through my own experiences and my interactions with Shapiro, I learned that identity is much more than an abstract concept—it is the connective tissue that binds members together, creating a sense of unity and shared destiny that is essential for a community's resilience and longevity. Identity is not just about having a name or a tagline—it's the heart of a community. It defines how people see themselves as part of something bigger and gives them a sense of belonging.

I've seen how important identity is in keeping a community together, especially when things get tough. Identity isn't conceptual—it gives people the feeling that they're connected, not just today but for the long term.

Shapiro's work in conflict resolution, particularly in post-conflict rebuilding, demonstrates that identity plays a pivotal role in fostering trust and cohesion, especially in situations where communities have been fragmented. Whether rebuilding war-torn nations or navigating the complexities of divided communities, it is often the reclamation of a shared identity that facilitates cooperation and mutual understanding. This process of re-forging a collective identity helps establish the foundation for long-term collaboration, mutual support, and the collective rebuilding of a resilient community. In the same way, community building in non-conflict contexts relies heavily on crafting a shared identity that members can rally around and sustain over time.

In the Global Shapers Community, identity was built on loyalty, symbols, and shared experiences. Loyalty comes from having meaningful experiences together, moments that bond people and make them feel part of something they genuinely care about. When people are loyal to a community, they stay involved, even when times are hard. This loyalty kept our community strong when we faced uncertainty or change.

One of the most powerful symbols in our community is the pinning ceremony. During the Global Shapers Summit, each Curator is pinned by another Shaper during the closing ceremony, and this isn't just a simple act. It is a meaningful ritual. The person doing the pinning explains why the Shaper deserves this honor. The pin symbolizes more than just attending the summit—it is a reminder that each person is part of something larger than themselves. This act of recognition makes people feel proud and committed to the community.

These symbols, like the pin, helped strengthen the Global Shapers' identity. They weren't just reminders of our achievements but signs of belonging and connection. When someone wore that pin, they knew they were part of a global movement. That sense of identity was crucial in keeping the community united.

But identity is also shaped by stories. Our shared history, moments of success, and even the challenges we overcame together created a mythos, or shared story, that everyone in the community could relate to. These stories became a part of who we were as a group. They reminded us of our journey and what we could accomplish together.

However, building a strong community identity isn't just about knowing who we are. It's also about how we feel within the group. In the book *Beyond Reason: Using Emotions as You Negotiate*, Daniel Shapiro, co-authored with Roger Fisher, shares a framework for building strong emotional ties. The framework identifies five core concerns that help build strong emotional ties: affiliation, appreciation, autonomy, role, and status. These concerns touch on basic human needs that, when met, can help a community grow and thrive.

Affiliation is the need to feel connected. People in a community need to bond with each other, share experiences, and build lasting relationships. The stronger these connections are, the more likely people will stick together when things get complicated. In the Global Shapers Community, creating opportunities for people to connect personally was vital to building that sense of belonging.

Appreciation is all about recognizing each person's contribution. People want to know that their efforts matter and that what they do is valued. In our community, we made sure to acknowledge both big and small achievements. Whether someone led a significant project or helped behind the scenes, their work was appreciated. This recognition motivated people to stay involved and continue contributing to the community's goals.

Autonomy is the freedom to make one's own choices. In a healthy community, members must feel they can take initiative, make decisions, and act without always needing approval. This sense of ownership drives people to stay engaged and feel responsible for the community's success. The more autonomy people have, the more invested they become in the community's future.

The role is about knowing where you fit in and how you contribute. People feel more confident and motivated when they understand their role in the community. Clear roles help prevent misunderstandings and allow the community to function smoothly. In the Global Shapers Community, we worked hard to ensure everyone knew their place and how their efforts helped move the community forward.

Status is about feeling respected. Everyone wants to think that their position in the group is recognized and valued. Whether through formal titles or informal recognition, acknowledging people's status helps maintain harmony in the community. It reassures them that their work is seen and that they matter.

In the Global Shapers Community, these emotional concerns were addressed in our daily interactions and governance structures. For example, symbols like the Global Shapers logo, the term "Shapers," and even hashtags like #ShapersLove helped create a unique identity. These small elements contributed to a sense of belonging and helped members stay emotionally connected to the community's mission.

By focusing on these core emotional concerns, we built a community where people were empowered to contribute to the community's success. This emotional connection made the community resilient, even in difficult times.

A strong community identity, then, is more than just words. It's the combination of shared purpose, symbols, and emotional bonds. When these elements come together, they create a community that isn't just functional but thriving. Whether through ceremonies like the pinning event or the deeper bonds of loyalty and shared stories, a strong identity is the foundation for any lasting impact a community can make.

Building a solid identity is one of the most essential parts of community building. It keeps people engaged, motivated, and ready to face challenges together. Without a clear identity, a community can quickly lose direction. But with it, there's no limit to what the group can achieve. The lessons learned from the Global Shapers Community and Forum of Young Global Leaders experiences are valuable for communities or groups looking to create a lasting impact. When people feel part of something meaningful, their emotional needs are met, and their contributions are valued, they are more likely to stay committed. And that's when the real work begins—building something that lasts.

CHAPTER 9:
PATHWAYS TO PURPOSE: THE THEORY OF CHANGE

"The work of today shapes the strength of tomorrow."
– Ibn Sina (Avicenna)

In a world increasingly defined by complex social, economic, and environmental challenges, communities, organizations, and leaders are tasked with crafting interventions that create lasting change. To do this effectively, they rely on the Theory of Change (ToC)—a systematic approach that outlines the steps required to move from vision to impact. This framework provides a roadmap grounded in evidence, purpose, and actionable steps, moving beyond mere goal-setting. By establishing clear pathways from the present state to a desired outcome, the Theory of Change enables organizations to not only envision the change they seek but to strategically align their actions to make it a reality.

A well-defined Theory of Change provides accountability, fosters cohesion, and creates a shared understanding of the journey towards impactful transformation. At its core, it asks: How do we get from where we are to where we want to be, and what conditions, resources, and changes are needed along the way?

To truly grasp the significance of the Theory of Change, it is essential to explore some of the foundational frameworks that have shaped this approach to social impact over the years. Each framework provides a distinct perspective on designing and implementing sustainable change, and together, they form a powerful toolkit for those seeking to build resilient communities and organizations.

One of the earliest models of Theory of Change is the Logical Framework Approach (LFA), developed in the 1960s by the United States Agency for International Development (USAID). As one of the first structured frameworks, LFA offers a systematic hierarchy of objectives, organizing activities to produce outputs, outputs to drive outcomes, and outcomes to lead to long-term impact. Through this organized progression, the LFA model offers clarity and accountability, making it particularly well-suited to project management in complex, resource-constrained environments. The framework relies on measurable indicators at each level to track progress, ensuring that all efforts align closely with the ultimate goal. However, the logical rigidity of LFA has drawn some criticism. Bakewell and Garbutt (2005) summarized the critics of the NGO and international development agencies in their publication "The Use and Abuse of the Logical Framework Approach". According to them, the LFA tends to assume a direct, linear relationship between actions and outcomes, a simplification that often doesn't hold in dynamic, community-based settings. For initiatives requiring adaptability and responsiveness—such as community-building projects—LFA's linear nature can sometimes limit flexibility, as it struggles to accommodate the spontaneous, evolving nature of social systems.

Recognizing the need for a more nuanced approach, John Mayne introduced a new concept in the Theory of Change landscape: Contribution Mapping. Unlike traditional models that emphasize attribution—the idea that specific actions directly cause specific outcomes—Contribution Mapping acknowledges that change is often the result of multiple overlapping efforts, influenced by a complex web of stakeholders, external factors, and contextual variables. This model is particularly useful in scenarios where the outcomes are affected by numerous actors and influences, such as public health or large-scale community initiatives. Rather than attempting to assign singular responsibility for results, Contribution Mapping helps organizations establish evidence-based connections between activities and the broader impact, enabling them to evaluate how plausible it is that their efforts are contributing meaningfully to desired outcomes. This model, with its emphasis on contribution rather than causation, is especially well-suited for projects embedded in complex social ecosystems, as it provides a realistic approach to understanding impact without oversimplifying causality.

Building on the ideas of Contribution Mapping, another powerful approach to Theory of Change emerged in the work of Sarah Earl, Fred Carden, and Terry Smutylo at the International Development Research Centre (IDRC). Known as Outcome Mapping, this model shifts the focus from end goals to behavioral changes among the people and organizations involved in or affected by an initiative. Unlike LFA, which tends to center on measurable outputs, Outcome Mapping values transformation in behaviors, relationships, and practices as indicators of progress. By tracking changes among "boundary partners"—key stakeholders who directly influence or are influenced by the project—Outcome Mapping acknowledges that sustainable impact is often rooted in human behavior and interpersonal dynamics. This model is particularly valuable for initiatives centered around community development, as it emphasizes the importance of engaging local stakeholders in meaningful ways, respecting their agency, and creating space for their unique contributions. Outcome Mapping recognizes that meaningful impact is more than achieving a static goal; it is about fostering a sustained shift in the attitudes and practices that shape a community's response to change.

Together, these models—LFA, Contribution Mapping, and Outcome Mapping—offer diverse yet complementary perspectives on the Theory of Change. While LFA provides a structured, measurable approach to organizing actions and outputs, Contribution Mapping and Outcome Mapping introduce a level of adaptability and nuance, acknowledging the complex, interdependent nature of real-world change. Each model brings valuable insights to the practice of Theory of Change, enabling organizations to tailor their strategies to fit the specific needs and dynamics of their projects.

A carefully crafted Theory of Change not only charts the steps from intention to impact but also invites stakeholders to participate in a collective vision, creating a shared foundation of accountability, adaptability, and intentionality. For a community-based initiative like the Global Shapers Community, the Theory of Change has served as an essential framework, helping young leaders around the world channel their passions and align their actions with measurable outcomes, all while remaining responsive to the unique needs of their local contexts.

In the following sections, we will explore how the Global Shapers Community has applied elements of these theoretical approaches, demonstrating the power of a well-defined Theory of Change in fostering dynamic, adaptive, and impactful change across communities globally. Through the stories and lessons drawn from this community, we will see the Theory of Change not as an abstract concept but as a lived philosophy that brings purpose and possibility to the pursuit of meaningful change.

As we explore the practical applications of Theory of Change, the Global Shapers Community offers a compelling, real-world example of this framework in action. Founded on principles that align with models like Contribution Mapping and Outcome Mapping, the Global Shapers' approach illustrates how a decentralized, youth-driven community can harness a Theory of Change to address local challenges with global significance. Through its adaptive structure, the Global Shapers Community demonstrates how a clear vision, coupled with an agile and layered framework, can empower young leaders to make meaningful, measurable change, one community at a time.

The community's mission centers on empowering young voices to create change, inspiring each member to take roles seriously as everyone works toward meaningful impact. This effort is not just a hopeful sentiment; it's structured around an intentional Impact Model, Theory of Change, and a detailed Indicator Framework, guiding every Shaper and hub to be impactful within their local communities and, collectively, on a global scale. Together, these frameworks equip everyone with the tools to track the progress, learn from the actions, and ensure tangible outcomes are being driven.

The Theory of Change within the Global Shapers Community embodies a vision that empowers young people to catalyze local and global transformation, grounded in a clear, actionable framework. The Community has become a leading example of how distributed, youth-led initiatives can yield measurable impact on global issues such as climate change, social justice, economic inclusion, and public health. With over 500 hubs worldwide and a growing network of 16,000 members and alumni, the community's Theory of Change is not only ambitious but also adaptive, reflecting the unique dynamics of each local hub while fostering a cohesive, impactful global movement.

The community's Theory of Change is based on four interdependent pillars: Global Shapers, Hubs, Local Communities, and the Global Network. Each of these elements forms a strategic component of the impact model, designed to empower young leaders to act within their immediate environments while maintaining a global vision. This multi-level framework ensures that each hub operates autonomously but within a unified mission, enabling projects to address urgent local issues with the potential to scale and inspire similar initiatives worldwide.

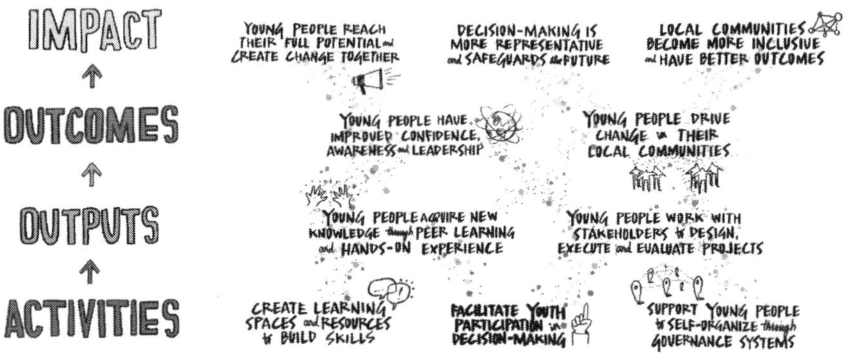

Global Shapers Community Theory of change.
Decade of impact report 2021

The first pillar, **Global Shapers**, recognizes each member as a vital contributor to their hub and the broader community. Members are encouraged to bring their unique skills, perspectives, and networks, fostering a culture of personal growth and peer learning. Through participation in events, activities, and collaborative projects, each Shaper develops skills and builds relationships that increase their capacity to drive change locally and globally.

The second pillar, **Hubs**, facilitates decentralization and autonomy. Each hub operates independently, identifying its own priorities and organizing projects that align with the specific needs of its community. This flexibility is vital to the community's Theory of Change, as it allows hubs to be agile, responsive, and contextually relevant. To support high performance, hubs are guided by principles of transparency, inclusivity, and collaboration, creating an environment where ideas can be incubated and translated into action.

Local Communities form the third pillar, representing the primary beneficiaries of the Global Shapers' efforts. Through projects tailored to address community-specific issues, Shapers can directly impact lives, whether by launching climate initiatives, providing digital literacy training, or advancing health equity. Each hub aims to execute at least one significant project annually, creating measurable benefits for the communities they serve. This community-centric focus ensures that impact remains meaningful, addressing needs as they arise within local contexts.

Finally, the **Global Network** serves as a platform for scaling impact. Once a hub's project gains traction and demonstrates success, it can be shared and replicated across other hubs worldwide. Events like the Global Shapers Community Annual Summit and the SHAPE regional events provide opportunities for cross-hub collaboration, fostering knowledge exchange and enabling hubs to adapt successful models to their own contexts. This interconnectedness exemplifies the community's Theory of Change, which relies on a global commitment to shared learning and innovation to magnify impact.

Over the past decade, the Theory of Change within the Global Shapers Community has evolved, informed by experience, ongoing evaluation, and the commitment to creating tangible, lasting outcomes. The community uses a comprehensive impact model, grounded in the Sustainable Development Goals (SDGs), to track and measure progress. Projects align with key SDGs, allowing the community to demonstrate how its initiatives contribute to global targets. Since 2017, the community has mobilized millions of people, trained hundreds of thousands, and influenced numerous policy changes, marking a clear, measurable path of impact.

The introduction of impact areas further clarifies the community's focus, enabling hubs to coordinate efforts on shared priorities while adapting to their unique environments. These impact areas which we call I-SHAPE: Inclusion, Skills, Health, Aid, Planet, and Engagement, provide a structured yet flexible framework that ensures the Theory of Change remains aligned with local needs and global goals. Young people can and should, lead on these issues, embracing the responsibility to build solutions that will last. We see these six areas as a reflection of the priorities that have been defined by the young generation—a roadmap that not only guides the actions but also represents the collective vision of the future they would like to see.

Inclusion is at the forefront. The community is driven by the commitment to create atmospheres where every voice matters and where diversity is celebrated. This means standing up for human rights and working against stereotypes that hold people back based on race, gender, disability, or any other identity.

The next impact area, **Skills**, focuses on preparing for the future. Shapers believe that everyone deserves access to quality education and skills training. In an era shaped by the fourth industrial revolution, the community is passionate about promoting digital literacy and online safety, equipping people with the tools they need for jobs in the modern world. The hubs organize training workshops, host coding boot camps, and create learning platforms that not only teach new skills but also boost confidence.

Health lies at the heart of everything the community does, and Shapers are committed to enhancing both mental and physical well-being within our communities. From expanding access to healthcare resources to raising awareness about youth mental health, the mission is to ensure health equity for all. Recent global health challenges underscored the importance of supporting one another in times of need, and the projects embody a proactive approach to wellness. Some hubs have even collaborated with local health organizations to offer mental health workshops, demonstrating how community-driven initiatives can play a vital role in advancing broader health efforts. One of the most impactful hub projects I witnessed, titled "It's Okay Not to Be Okay" by the Kuala Lumpur Hub, resonated with me profoundly, underscoring the power of breaking taboos about mental health, all while opening dialogue and offering support mechanisms.

Aid focuses on delivering essential support and addressing the immediate needs of the most vulnerable populations. In times of crisis, whether disasters, food insecurity, or deep-seated poverty—action cannot wait. Through this pillar, the hubs often step in to provide life-changing humanitarian assistance. One of the most memorable experiences I had was during SHAPE Latin America, where 200 Shapers gathered in São Paulo's favelas to transform a local school. From the moment we arrived, the atmosphere was electric—Shapers from hubs across the continent rolled up their sleeves, each determined to make an impact. Over a single day, we repainted walls that had long faded, restored a neglected garden to lush life, cleared away heaps of rubbish, and brought laughter back to the school's hallways with activities for the kids. It was more than just a project; it was a festival of hope and unity. Every brushstroke, every garden spade, and every laugh with the children reminded us of the strength of collective action. By the end of the day, the school stood transformed, not only in appearance but as a testament to what a community of hands and hearts can achieve. It was humbling and inspiring—a moment that truly captured the spirit of what it means to be a Shaper.

The work under **Planet** highlights the commitment to environmental sustainability. Protecting our planet goes beyond just talking about climate change; it's about taking actionable steps. Many hubs are engaged in projects aimed at reducing emissions, promoting sustainable lifestyles, and conserving resources. It's about accountability, holding ourselves and our leaders responsible for the environmental future we want to build. In 2015, under the leadership of Yemi Babington-Ashaye, former Head of the Global Shapers Community, the community launched its first Global Shapers Survey, quickly becoming a powerful reflection of the concerns and hopes of young leaders worldwide. Over the years, the survey grew, and the latest editions have gathered more than 30,000 responses from both within and beyond the community. A particularly striking trend emerged over three consecutive years, one that highlighted a disconnect we knew we had to address.

Two questions became focal points: "What is the top priority at the local level?" and "What is your top priority at the global level?" For the local question, responses predominantly focused on education, unemployment, and health—immediate, tangible challenges that communities felt urgently needed attention. But when asked about priorities at the global level, climate change was almost universally cited as the top concern. It was as though climate change was seen as an essential issue, yet one left for "someone else" to tackle, as if each of us were silently hoping another would take on the responsibility.

Realizing this gap in accountability, we knew we had to shift from merely acknowledging climate concerns to actively addressing them within our community. We partnered with the Climate Reality Project, creating a platform to train Shapers and give the resources that enabled hubs worldwide to engage in environmental action. From a standing start, our projects addressing climate change rose from zero to over 200 by my last year as Head of the Community, marking a powerful shift from intention to tangible impact.

The **Engagement** pillar brings us to the heart of participation. When we push for civic involvement, it goes beyond just encouraging people to vote; it's about showing young people that their voices matter in every layer of decision-making, whether it's a community meeting or a global forum. Every time we create a space for youth voices in local or international policies, we're sending a message: this generation is essential, and our perspectives belong at the table. Ensuring fair representation in these spaces isn't just a goal—it's a commitment. And through this, we help our community members, especially the younger ones, realize that they, too, have a voice that deserves to be heard.

The work follows a structured path, a roadmap, a guide to the journey from what we plan to achieve to the tangible difference we hope to make. Every part of it connects, step-by-step, from the initial inputs to the lasting impact. To keep everyone on track, the community uses an Indicator Framework to give clear markers of what is being achieved. It's not about just moving forward blindly; instead, it's about collecting data, analyzing it, and using it to refine every approach. It's powerful to know that every action, every workshop, every project has a place in this larger vision, contributing piece by piece to the bigger picture of change we're building together.

One of the most meaningful ways to measure success is through the stories and the numbers. How many people did the efforts directly benefit? How many organizations, like local NGOs or schools, felt the impact of the work? Each of these numbers represents real lives touched, communities supported, and connections strengthened. Each class taught, each donation made, and each workshop held adds up to a broader impact. Social media pledges and other online efforts may look like just numbers, but they signify a reach beyond physical limits, extending the mission's influence on people who may never set foot in our hubs.

The Community's Theory of Change lays out a structured approach with four levels, each bringing us closer to our final goal. The first level, Activities, includes all the actions we take, like offering trainings, sharing resources, or organizing summits. These aren't just busy tasks; they're carefully planned steps that empower the members to lead change within their own communities. These activities are meant to support Shapers, equipping them with everything they need to execute projects and create impact where it's needed.

From these activities come Outputs—the tangible results. These outputs include the new skills the members acquire, the platforms where their voices are heard, and the projects that start to take shape in communities. It's an exciting phase because it's here that we see the first signs of the work taking root. Each new skill, each local project, each collaboration across hubs shows the real progress from our initial actions.

We see young people gaining confidence, becoming more vocal, and, most importantly, feeling empowered.

The third level, Outcomes, reflects the changes that come as a direct result of the outputs. When Shapers acquire new leadership skills and see the impact of their work, we begin to notice shifts in how they approach challenges and collaborate. The changes don't just happen within them—they ripple outwards. Decision-making becomes more inclusive, and communities start noticing the value of engaging youth perspectives.

And finally, we reach Impact—the long-term difference we set out to make. This is the peak, where all the efforts come together to ensure that young people play a critical role in shaping their present and future. The aim isn't just to make a difference for today but to lay a foundation for future generations. We want to reach a place where youth involvement is not exceptional or optional but expected, where their role in decision-making is seen as essential. This is the ultimate goal, the vision that motivates each one of us as we push forward.

We've created a framework with 36 indicators across these levels to support this Theory of Change. These indicators give everyone a clear picture of what we're achieving and where we're going. They help us keep the vision grounded in reality, showing us the real impact of the actions. Each indicator is like a checkpoint, reminding everyone to evaluate the steps and adjust as needed. By monitoring these, we ensure the journey is aligned with our mission. Below are all the indicators:

Activities	What are we going to measure?	How are we going to measure? (Performance Indicators)
We create opportunities for diverse changemakers to build skills	1.1. Learning spaces and skills building resources are available for Shapers	1.1.1. # of skills building resources available to Shapers
		1.1.2. # of learning spaces available to Shapers
		1.1.3. # of Shapers who benefited from resources (courses)
		1.1.4. # of Shapers who benefited from learning spaces (events)
	1.2. Growing membership for increased networking, peer exchange and development	1.2.1. Total # of Shapers
		1.2.2. Average # of Shapers per hub
		1.2.3. Total # of Alumni
	1.3. Diverse membership for increased growth and understanding	1.3.1. Shaper membership profiles are diverse (including gender, race and ethnic background, persons with a disability, age, education, work experience and industry)
We facilitate youth participation in decision-making spaces	2.1. Opportunities for Shapers to participate in decision-making	2.1.1. # of Shapers who participate in international decision-making events
We support young people to self-organize to lead impactful projects	3.1. Shapers are organized in hubs	3.1.1. Total # of countries
		3.1.2. Total # of hubs
		3.1.3. # of hubs opened
		3.1.4. # of hubs closed
	3.2. Shapers are supported to create and execute projects	3.2.1. # of projects supported (funding or mentorship)
		3.2.2. Amount of funding distributed
		3.2.3. # of GSC partners
Outputs	**What are we going to measure?**	**How are we going to measure? (Performance Indicators)**
Young people acquire new skills to lead and influence others	1.1. Shapers gain skills	1.1.3. % of Shapers that have significantly or very significantly improved their skills after becoming a Shaper

Diverse youth voices are amplified on a global scale	2.1. Shapers have their voice amplified	2.1.1. # of Shapers who participate in speaking opportunities that facilitate their input into decision-making processes (official panel role or closed discussion groups)
		2.1.2. # of Shapers who publish an article on the Forum Agenda
		2.1.3. # of Shapers that are part of Forum Councils, initiatives or discussion groups
		2.1.4. % of Shapers across regions who had their voices amplified
Young people self-organize to deliver projects to address local needs	3.1. Shapers design and execute projects	3.1.1. # of hub projects executed in the year
		3.1.2. # of active cross-hub initiatives in the year
	3.2. Shapers self-organize in an inclusive space	3.2.1. Young people self-organize within their hub through regular hub meetings
		3.2.2. % of Shapers that agree that their hub is inclusive, equitable, engaging, safe and fair
Outcomes	**What are we going to measure?**	**How are we going to measure? (Performance Indicators)**
Young people have the confidence and capability to advocate for their interests	1.1. Shapers apply their acquired skills for change	1.1.2. % of Shapers who confirm their improved skills gave them greater confidence and increased ability to create change
Decision-making is more representative of current and future generations	2.1. Shapers participate in policy-related decision-making	2.1.2. # of Shapers who have served in high-level leadership positions (i.e. political appointment, managerial position in a company or civil society organization) within the last year

Young people contribute to positive and lasting change with diverse stakeholders	3.1. Diverse stakeholders are included in the change	3.1.1. % of Shapers who confirm that stakeholders were included in the (i) design, (ii) execution and (iii) evaluation for a certain % of hub projects
		3.1.2. The % breakdown of total hub project stakeholders is diverse (i.e. reflects more than one demographic)
		3.1.3. % of hubs that created partnerships with at least one type of actor within their community in the execution of their work
	3.2. Shapers effectively leading projects for positive change	3.2.1. # of hubs that are tracking their project success using or aligned to the SDG framework, another international standard or their own framework.
Impact	**What are we going to measure?**	**How are we going to measure? (Performance Indicators)**
Young people are playing a critical role in shaping their present and future	1.1. Young people are influencing critical decision-making bodies	1.1.1. # of projects per year that achieve policy change
	1.2. Local communities are seeing better outcomes	1.2.1. # of people in their local communities who directly benefitted from hub projects
		1.2.2. # of people in their local communities who were reached and mobilized by hub projects (excluding people who directly benefited)
		1.2.3. Change has been achieved in a diversity of areas
		1.2.4. Change has been achieved in local communities in different forms

CHAPTER 10:
COMMUNITY GOVERNANCE: THE LEADERSHIP

Community is much more than belonging to something; it's about doing something together that makes belonging matter."
– Brian Solis

A community's leadership model acts as a heartbeat—steady, open, and collaborative, guiding everyone forward with purpose. Every part of this structure works together seamlessly to keep the community vibrant and mission-aligned. Leaders don't just direct from the top; they create a governance system that values input at all levels, fostering collaboration and empowering every member. This approach strengthens the community, uniting everyone under shared goals while ensuring that each voice is heard and valued. A prime example of this approach in action is the Global Shapers Community, where governance lies at the core of its success and resilience.

At the center of this structure is the Foundation Board, which sets the community's vision and high-level priorities guiding the collective efforts. The board comprises leaders from business, government, and, importantly, from the community itself. The board members meet twice a year—at the World Economic Forum Annual Meeting in Davos and again at the Global Shapers Annual Meeting. In these meetings, they gather to chart the course for the collective goals.

With prominent figures such as Professor Klaus Schwab, Founder and Chairman of the World Economic Forum, alongside notable members like Her Royal Highness the Crown Princess of Norway; Jack Ma, Founder and former Executive Chairman of Alibaba Group; and David Rubenstein, Co-Founder and Co-Chairman of The Carlyle Group, the board brings a wealth of experience and insights. This range of perspectives supports a comprehensive and impactful approach to guiding the community toward its mission.

I remember listening to a discussion during one meeting about community expansion and realizing how each board member brought with them their unique background. "We have to ensure this expansion reaches even all world capitals even if they are small cities," someone said, emphasizing inclusivity in every decision. This moment underscored the board's commitment to keeping our vision broad but grounded. Every board member knows that while setting goals is essential, supporting each hub is what keeps the community growing.

While the board defines the larger vision, the Global Shapers HQ leads the day-to-day operations as the executive force behind our community's efforts. Located in Geneva, Switzerland, and hosted by the World Economic Forum, the headquarters is small but mighty. This team is the engine that keeps everything running, from event organization to community support. I often picture the HQ as a well-organized control tower, with each team member managing their region or specialization. The Head of the Global Shapers Community leads with a clear vision, coordinating efforts with team members representing diverse global regions. Their roles go far beyond administration—they're the cohesive force that unites the worldwide community. I would like to take this opportunity to recognize all Heads of the Global Shapers Community chronologically: David Aikman, Yemi Babington-Ashaye, myself, and since 2022, Natalie Pierce.

I've had the privilege of working closely with many members of the HQ team, both past and present, and their dedication and passion constantly inspire me. Each person brings unique skills to the table—whether ensuring engagements across different regions, overseeing thematic portfolios, managing events, or countless other responsibilities. Together, they form the backbone of the community, each contributing to the crucial mission in essential ways. Their commitment to creating a lasting impact has been both unwavering and contagious to make our collective vision a reality. I'm profoundly grateful for their hard work and the spirit they bring to this mission every day. To you: Abdullahi, Adrian, Albina, Ana, Anastasia, Antonio, Brittany, Chidiogo, David, James, Johann, Gauhar, Katie, Karen, Karine, Kenza, Manuel, Matthew, Melih, Michael, Murray, Natalie, Noa, Olympia, Pierre, Raissa, Shimer, Sophia, Spring, Vera, Vijay, Weiyuan, Yemi, and of course to the extended team that supports us from behind the scenes.

Another important pillar of any community's governance is Advisory Councils. It embodies the belief that governance should be inclusive, with community members or stakeholders actively participating in decision-making. In the Global Shapers Community, around fifteen members serve on the committee, volunteering their time each month to uphold the values, oversee elections and conflicts, and enhance engagement. These council members bridge the gap between HQ and the broader community, ensuring everyone's voice is heard. I often think of them as our community's advocates or ambassadors, bringing the grassroots perspective into our governance structure and vice versa.

The dedication of the council members is impressive. Each month, they dedicate 10 to 15 hours to strengthening the community, not because they're obligated to but because they genuinely desire to see it thrive. I once asked one of the council members what kept him motivated, and he said, "This community has given me so much; giving back feels like the natural thing to do." This sense of responsibility and belonging makes the Advisory Council an essential part of our leadership model.

The Community Champions support all these elements and extend the Advisory Council's reach across every region. Community Champions are selected from the most experienced community members, including founding curators, curators, and alumni. These Champions are vital in offering one-on-one support to hubs worldwide, ensuring each one feels connected and supported. Acting as mentors and trusted advisors, they help address challenges and scale best practices, strengthening activities across the globe. Community Champions are, in a way, the unsung heroes, always ready to step in and provide guidance wherever needed, especially when the Community Managers at HQ are overstretched or cannot attend in person.

The impact of the Community Champions can be felt in every hub they support. They are there to offer advice, lend a listening ear, and share the insights they've gained over years of experience. Most importantly, they are locally based, which means they are close to the Shapers and can pay attention to the details that HQ can't attend to daily. Sometimes, it's just about being there to listen and guide the hubs. Their presence ensures that no hub feels isolated, even if it's miles away from others. They create a safety net for each hub, allowing every member to thrive in a supportive environment.

Steering Committees like the one dedicated to Climate Action form another essential layer in the governance structure, embodying our community's commitment to tackling global challenges collaboratively. These committees bring together experts and dedicated members from across the network who share a focused mission, such as advancing sustainable solutions to address climate change. They work tirelessly behind the scenes, leveraging their expertise and networks to drive impactful initiatives, from raising awareness on environmental issues to coordinating global campaigns.

The Climate Action Steering Committee, for instance, is a hub of energy, ideas, and action. Its members aren't just passive contributors—they are active changemakers who set ambitious goals and mobilize resources across hubs worldwide. Each member understands the urgent need for climate action and brings their unique skills to the table, be it through partnerships, policy advocacy, or on-the-ground projects. Their shared commitment keeps the momentum alive and inspires other community members to take concrete steps in their own regions.

Steering committees can also be ad hoc, like the one we created in the aftermath of COVID-19. This specific committee worked tirelessly to produce a report on pressing issues young people faced during the pandemic, capturing the voices and concerns of youth from around the world. Through widespread virtual dialogues and surveys, they gathered insights on the pandemic's impact across ten key areas—such as digital access, mental health, and inclusive job opportunities—and proposed actionable recommendations. This initiative, known as the Davos Lab: Youth Recovery Plan, included over 340 dialogues in 146 cities and engaged more than 19,000 participants.

The ad hoc committee's commitment resulted in a comprehensive report with 40 policy recommendations aimed at addressing youth challenges in the post-pandemic world. They advocated for a fairer and more resilient society, emphasizing sustainable development, digital equity, mental health support, and economic security. Their efforts underscored the importance of empowering young people to lead transformative action and provided a structured platform for youth to shape policies, ensuring that future crisis responses consider the unique needs and perspectives of the younger generation.

Together, these different elements of community leadership—the Foundation Board, Global Shapers HQ, Advisory Council, Community Champions, and Steering Committees—

make up a flexible, inclusive, and robust system. Each part of this governance model supports the others, ensuring the community is well-guided, connected, and driven by a shared purpose. This collaborative leadership structure allows adaptation to new challenges and provides a strong foundation for continued growth, always centered around the mission.

CHAPTER 11: **CURATING COMMITMENT: BEING A SHAPER**

"A tree with strong roots laughs at storms."
– Malaysian Proverb

In any thriving community, there's a delicate balance between fostering organic connections and establishing clear processes that guide, support, and uplift its members. The structure, the standards, and the shared understanding all work together to create a space where individuals not only feel they belong but are also empowered to contribute meaningfully. Having well-thought-out processes in place is essential—it's these invisible threads that hold a community together, providing continuity, inclusivity, and a shared sense of purpose. Here it is, the Global Shaper Way.

At the heart of the Global Shapers Community lies the Charter, a foundational document that serves as a compass for every member. It is more than a list of rules; it's a declaration of our collective values, a commitment to the principles that define who we are and why we're here. The Charter lays out responsibilities, expectations, and guiding principles, setting a standard that every Shaper aspires to uphold. It's a reminder that by joining this community, each person commits to bring their best each and every day, dedicating themselves to ongoing growth and vowing to make a lasting impact. It binds all stakeholders together in a common purpose, providing a roadmap for every member's journey.

This journey begins with recruitment, and here, the Global Shapers Community takes a unique approach. Each local hub is responsible for its own recruitment process, ensuring that new members are chosen by those who know the needs and character of the hub best. It's a decentralized system that respects the autonomy of each hub while upholding the core values outlined in the Charter. Recruitment isn't simply about filling seats; it's about finding individuals who are aligned with the community's mission, who bring diverse perspectives, and who are committed to engaging actively. Every hub carries out recruitment at least once a year, often viewing each new member as if they were filling the final, most essential spot. It's a process grounded in intention, one that brings together individuals ready to serve.

Selection committees within each hub, composed of current members, lead the recruitment effort. They're responsible for evaluating applications, conducting interviews, and making decisions that shape the hub's future. There's beauty in watching this process unfold across different hubs, each with its own culture yet united by a shared mission. Every step, from the first contact with potential candidates to the final decision, should be handled with care. Some hubs choose to run recruitment cycles, creating an atmosphere of excitement around the "selection season." Others opt for a year-round approach, allowing for a more flexible integration of new members. Regardless of the method, the focus remains the same: selecting people who resonate with the community's purpose.

This decentralized recruitment approach is quite distinct from other communities, such as the Young Global Leaders (YGL) Community, where members are nominated by third parties rather than applying directly. For YGLs, the process is centralized and highly selective, with the World Economic Forum Headquarters evaluating thousands of nominations from across the globe. Only around 100 candidates are chosen each year—a rigorous selection process that results in a small, curated group of leaders. There's no self-nomination in YGL; instead, members are identified for their exceptional leadership and contributions, often before they even consider applying themselves. This centralized model works well for YGL's goals, creating a community of established leaders recognized by others in their field. In contrast, the Global Shapers model celebrates self-nomination, inviting young people to step forward, showcase their passion, and claim their space in the community.

Once selected, new Shapers embark on an onboarding journey that introduces them to the hub's culture, projects, and the larger Global Shapers network. This is more than a formal orientation; it's a process designed to instill a sense of belonging and commitment from day one. Many hubs host induction days, where new members meet their peers, learn about ongoing projects, and get acquainted with the community's mission. This local onboarding is complemented by access to the global platform, where Shapers from around the world connect, share ideas, and collaborate on initiatives. For a new Shaper, joining the platform is a momentous step, a gateway to a network that spans continents and cultures, united by a shared vision.

But becoming a Global Shaper is not a passive experience. Members are encouraged to actively participate in at least one project or leadership role each year. This expectation isn't about fulfilling a quota; it's an invitation to immerse oneself in the community, to grow through action, and to make a tangible impact. Projects vary across hubs—some focus on local issues, others address global challenges—but each project is an opportunity for Shapers to bring their unique skills to the table, to lead, and to learn. This active engagement is the heartbeat of the community, keeping it dynamic, responsive, and impactful.

Flexibility is another core aspect of the Global Shapers experience. If a member relocates, they can request a transfer to another hub, ensuring continuity in their Shapers journey. This fluidity strengthens the community, allowing members to stay connected to the mission no matter where life takes them. I've seen members transfer from hub to hub, welcomed with open arms each time, reinforcing the sense of global unity that defines the Shapers community. However, some hubs may establish guidelines, such as probation periods, to ensure that transferring members align with local goals and culture. This careful balance between openness and hub autonomy keeps the community adaptable yet cohesive.

Of course, maintaining a community like this requires accountability. The Global Shapers Charter sets clear expectations, and members commit to upholding these values throughout their journey. When someone struggles to meet these commitments, hubs provide guidance, allowing time for members to realign with the community's principles. In cases of serious misconduct, curators—and at a later stage, if not solved, the Advisory Council or the Global Shapers HQ—may step in to uphold the standards of integrity and respect that are foundational to the community. It's a structure designed not to punish but to preserve the trust and safety of the network, ensuring that every member contributes positively.

As members age out of the community, they automatically transition to alumni status, joining an ever-growing network of former Shapers who continue to support the mission in new ways. Alumni remain deeply connected, often returning to mentor current members, offer advice, or collaborate on projects. There's a saying in the community: "Once a Shaper, always a Shaper." This isn't just a slogan—it's a reflection of members' lifelong commitment, even as they move on to other phases of their lives.

Through each stage of this journey, from recruitment to alumni engagement, the Global Shapers Community demonstrates the power of intentional governance. It's a model that values every voice, respects every contribution, and cultivates a sense of belonging that endures. This journey—guided by the Charter, shaped by shared values, and sustained through engagement—is what keeps the community strong, resilient, and deeply impactful.

Global Shapers Community values voted on during the Annual Curators Meeting in 2015

In the art of curating communities, governance is not a burden but a gift. It's the framework that allows a group of diverse individuals to come together as one, bound by purpose and empowered to create change. By thoughtfully shaping each stage of membership, the Global Shapers Community has built a resilient, compassionate network that stands as a model for others. This journey of belonging is what transforms a collection of individuals into a true community—a constellation of people each shining in their unique way, yet united in the pursuit of a brighter future.

CHAPTER 12: COMMUNITY GOVERNANCE: CONFLICT RESOLUTION

"A bridge is built from both sides."
– African Proverb

I've come to learn—sometimes the hard way—that conflict is an inevitable aspect of any community, especially the ones that thrive on diversity, inclusion, and collective action. Whether arising from interpersonal dynamics, cultural differences, governance issues, or external pressures, conflicts are not only natural but sometimes necessary. They challenge assumptions, disrupt the status quo, and, when addressed constructively, create space for deeper understanding and comprehension. As someone who has navigated multiple roles between education, the corporate world, and international organizations, I've come to view conflict not as a threat but as an opportunity—one that, when handled effectively, can strengthen the very fabric of a community.

No community is immune to challenges, and my journey—both personal and professional—has shown me that conflict resolution is a critical component of any leader's toolkit. What sets resilient communities apart is their ability to address challenges proactively, turning points of contention into opportunities for collective growth. Effective governance plays a crucial role here, providing a structural framework where conflicts are not merely resolved but are used as catalysts for building trust, reinforcing shared values, and fostering unity. The key to effective conflict resolution is not simply to settle disputes but to use these moments to deepen understanding, strengthen relationships, and build a more cohesive community. Several conflict resolution mechanisms and theories provide valuable insights into how this can be achieved, particularly drawing from the work of renowned authors and practitioners like Chris Voss and George Kohlrieser. The next sections explore conflict resolution as an opportunity to deepen understanding, strengthen bonds, and fortify the community's foundation.

I've learned about the work of Chris Voss, a former FBI hostage negotiator, from the amazing Adam Grant, author and YGL, who highly spoke of Voss' work. One of the books he recommended was *Never Split the Difference,* where he introduces powerful negotiation techniques that can be effectively applied within community governance. One of the cornerstone concepts Voss emphasizes is tactical empathy—the ability to understand and articulate the emotions and perspectives of all parties involved in a conflict. By genuinely acknowledging and validating each member's feelings, leaders can create a foundation of trust and openness that facilitates more effective resolution.

Another key technique from Voss is mirroring, which involves subtly reflecting the speaker's words and emotions to build rapport and encourage them to share more information. This technique helps uncover the underlying interests and concerns that may drive the conflict, allowing for solutions that address the root causes rather than just the surface symptoms. Labelling—identifying and naming emotions—also helps defuse tension and makes all parties feel heard and understood. For example, a leader might say, "It sounds like you're feeling frustrated about the recent changes," thereby acknowledging the member's emotional state and opening the door for constructive dialogue.

It's paramount to listen actively to identify and name emotions. One technique I've learnt that helps with listening and empathy is Otto Scharmer's four listening levels: Downloading, Factual Listening, Empathic Listening, and Generative Listening. These levels have profoundly influenced how I approach working or interacting with people. They have shown me the depth to which leaders can connect with others.

At the most basic level of Downloading, we listen from our perspective, only hearing what confirms our beliefs. Many leaders begin here, especially in the early stages of their journey. I started here, too, simply reaffirming what I already knew. But as I grew, I learned that this kind of listening limits real connection and understanding.

The next level, Factual Listening, is where we start recognizing new data or ideas that don't necessarily align with our own. It's a step forward but still distant, focused more on information than the individual behind it. Even though I was open to new facts, it wasn't until I moved beyond this level that I genuinely connected with those around me.

The fundamental transformation comes when we embrace Empathic Listening. This is the level where we truly put ourselves in another person's shoes, feeling their emotions and understanding their experiences. When I applied this in my work, everything changed. It was no longer about simply hearing the words—it was about connecting with the feelings and seeing the world from the perspective of the other. When people feel genuinely seen and valued, they open up in ways that lead to robust engagement. This is where trust is built and where communities come alive.

But Scharmer's final level, Generative Listening, takes empathy even further. This is where leaders listen to understand or empathize and create something new together, especially after conflicts. It's listening with the intention of co-creating a shared future. This is where true breakthroughs happen.

I had the chance to meet George Kohlrieser, author of the famous book, *Hostage at the Table,* as he was invited to share with us his negotiation and conflict resolution work as part of the Global Leadership Fellowship at the World Economic Forum. In his work, Kohlrieser explores the importance of establishing trust and presence in high-stakes situations, drawing parallels to community leadership. Kohlrieser emphasizes the concept of Secure Base Leadership, where leaders provide a sense of safety and stability, much like a secure base from which members can explore and take risks without fear of judgment or retribution. This approach is vital in conflict resolution, as it encourages members to engage openly and honestly, knowing that their vulnerabilities will be respected and protected.

Kohlrieser also highlights the significance of active listening and authentic communication. By being fully present and attentive during discussions, leaders can better understand the nuances of each conflict and respond in ways that are both empathetic and effective. This presence fosters an environment where members feel valued and supported, making navigating disagreements and finding mutually beneficial solutions easier.

By incorporating negotiation techniques and trust-building strategies into governance structures, a community can enhance its conflict-resolution capabilities significantly. Here's how these mechanisms can be integrated:

1. **Tactical Empathy and Active Listening:** Encourage leaders and members to practice tactical empathy and active listening during conflicts. Training sessions or workshops based on Voss's techniques can equip members with the skills to effectively understand and articulate each other's perspectives. Otto Scharmer's four listening levels can also be very helpful here.
2. **Mirroring and Labeling:** Implement mirroring and labelling as standard practices in meetings and conflict discussions.

This ensures that all parties feel heard and that their emotions are acknowledged, paving the way for more meaningful and productive conversations.

3. **Secure Base Leadership:** Adopt the principles of Secure Base Leadership by creating governance policies that prioritize psychological safety. Leaders should model vulnerability and openness, demonstrating that it is safe to express concerns and disagreements without fear of negative consequences.

4. **Transparent Communication Channels:** Establish clear and transparent communication channels where conflicts can be aired and addressed promptly. This includes regular check-ins, feedback loops, and designated forums for discussing and resolving disputes.

5. **Training and Development:** Provide ongoing training for leaders and members of governance bodies on effective conflict resolution techniques. This investment in skill development ensures that the community is well-equipped to handle conflicts constructively.

6. **Structured Conflict Resolution Protocols:** Develop and formalize conflict resolution protocols within governance bodies. These protocols should clarify roles and responsibilities, specifying who initiates contact, who is involved in decision-making, and which steps are followed at each stage of the conflict. Clear guidelines should outline when issues should escalate to higher levels, such as the leadership team or the board, ensuring that conflicts are managed efficiently and appropriately. It's also important to have an appeal process. This helps create consistency and transparency, reassuring members that a reliable, fair process is in place.

7. **Feedback Mechanisms**: Establish feedback mechanisms to evaluate the effectiveness of conflict resolution processes regularly. By gathering input from members involved in or

affected by conflicts, governance bodies can identify areas for improvement and refine their approaches, promoting continuous learning and adaptation within the community.

By integrating these advanced conflict resolution mechanisms into its governance framework, a community ensures that conflicts are not only managed but also transformed into opportunities for deeper understanding and stronger connections. This proactive approach prevents conflicts from festering, preserving the community's integrity and reinforcing trust among its members. It fosters an environment where differences are respected and where dialogue can lead to innovation and growth. In this way, conflict resolution becomes an integral part of maintaining the health and cohesion of the community, ensuring that it remains a safe and supportive space for all members.

In the art of curating a community, servant leadership and governance are two sides of the same coin. While servant leadership provides the moral and ethical compass, governance offers the structural integrity that allows the community to grow, adapt, and flourish. Together, they create a resilient, dynamic environment where every member is empowered to contribute to a shared vision of impact.

The Global Shapers Community exemplifies how these elements can be seamlessly integrated to create a community that is not only effective in achieving its goals but also enduring in its relevance and influence. By embracing both servant leadership and governance, leaders can build communities that can make a lasting difference in the world, inspiring others to follow in their footsteps and continue the journey toward a better, more inclusive future.

That being said, creating a safe space in a community isn't just about handling conflicts when they arise. It's about building an environment where people feel valued daily and know their ideas and feelings matter. It's about being present, listening deeply, and showing care. This kind of leadership helps build trust, and trust is the foundation that holds everything else together.

However, trust is not a one-time achievement; it must be nurtured continuously. Trust grows through small actions—like keeping promises, being consistent, and being transparent. I've always believed that if you want people to trust you, you must first show that you trust them. That's why I've never been a fan of micromanaging. I prefer to give people the space to make decisions and learn from their experiences.

Trust and empathy are more powerful than authority. You can't force people to follow you; you can only inspire them to believe in your vision. And that belief comes when people see you're leading with their best interests at heart. This is the first step to solving any conflict even before it happens.

CHAPTER 13: **BUILDING TRUST**

"Knowledge without action is wastefulness and action without knowledge is foolishness."
– Imam Ghazali

Trust is the foundation of any thriving community. It is the thread that binds people together, creating a sense of safety and belonging. Trust isn't just about believing in someone; it's about knowing that everyone's contributions matter and their voices will be heard. It creates an environment where people feel empowered to share their thoughts without fear, take risks, and collaborate openly. Trust allows individuals to be vulnerable, knowing they'll be supported, and it helps turn ideas into collective action.

In my journey with the Global Shapers Community, trust was the invisible force that made everything possible, especially during challenging times. Whether facing a crisis or working on initiatives aimed at social impact, trust was always the key. It allowed people from different backgrounds and perspectives to unite with a shared purpose. Without trust, even the best strategies can fail, but with it, we can move forward confidently, no matter how uncertain the path is. I saw how trust enabled quick mobilization during critical moments, allowing us to support each other and achieve more together than we could individually.

Trust, however, isn't something that appears, as briefly mentioned earlier. It's built through consistent actions, transparency, and a commitment to the group's well-being. I believe that transparency breeds trust. This means being open about decisions, explaining their reasons, and ensuring everyone feels informed can help cultivate trust. When people know why choices are made—even difficult ones—it creates a sense of inclusion and respect. For me, transparency means no one is left guessing or feeling sidelined; everyone becomes part of an open dialogue that is intended to move the community forward.

Reflecting on my experiences, three pillars of trust stood out: reliability, openness, and accountability. Reliability is about being dependable. When people know they can count on each other, confidence grows. Actions should align with words such as showing up when expected or following through on commitments. It's a simple principle but incredibly powerful in building trust within a team.

Openness is about maintaining honest communication and creating a space where people feel comfortable speaking up. It is crucial to keep the lines of communication open, invite feedback, and ensure everyone's thoughts have a stake in the process. This openness helps foster a sense of shared ownership, making people feel more connected to the outcomes.

Accountability is equally important. It's not about placing blame; it's about taking responsibility. If something goes wrong, it's important for a leader to own up. This principle builds respect and shows commitment to high standards. This approach was particularly significant when we faced tough decisions, like closing some Global Shapers hubs that weren't meeting our community's values. It wasn't an easy process, but it reinforced the importance of holding ourselves and each other accountable to sustain the integrity of the mission.

One of the most challenging yet defining moments in my leadership journey came during the crisis in Afghanistan as mentioned before. Many of our Global Shapers were in immediate danger as the country deteriorated. It was a time of intense fear and uncertainty, and it was a time when the power of trust shone through. We had to rely on each other's judgment, skills, and commitment to the cause. Each person was vital in our collective efforts to support and coordinate evacuations. It was not just about logistics; it was about trusting that we would do everything possible to help those in need.

In those critical hours, I knew the strength of our bonds. Trusting the team meant I could focus on my part, knowing others would do the same. It wasn't about individual efforts but knowing that the same goal united everyone. This trust allowed us to overcome our challenges, providing much-needed support and hope to those in danger.

Building trust in culturally diverse environments takes a delicate balance of sensitivity, openness, and a genuine effort to understand the unique perspectives shaping each person's worldview. It's not just about acknowledging diversity but about celebrating it. It's about creating spaces where everyone, regardless of background, feels valued and heard.

This inclusivity must extend beyond formal settings. I strive to be consistent in how I interact with people, whether speaking with a government official or engaging with a young leader. Trust cannot be limited to certain situations; it must be a universal approach. Everyone deserves the same respect, and it's through these consistent actions that trust is built over time.

One early lesson in my leadership journey was realizing that building trust often requires exceeding expectations. Many believe that meeting someone halfway is enough, but I've found that genuine connection often requires more than that. It's about putting in extra effort—going 80% of the way rather than expecting both sides to meet perfectly in the middle. This approach has helped me connect deeply with people from different backgrounds, showing them that I am willing to meet them where they are.

My approach remains consistent whether I'm sharing tea with locals in Sanaa, Yemen, in Manaus, Brazil, or engaging with high-level officials in Armenia. I strive to honor the traditions and cultures of those I meet while staying true to my values. People appreciate this consistency because it shows that I am genuine and authentic. It's not about changing who I am to fit different settings; it's about respecting others while being myself. This authenticity is what makes trust possible.

One of the most rewarding aspects of this approach has been seeing how young leaders from different backgrounds respond to me in various settings. Whether we're meeting in SHAPE Africa in Nairobi or navigating the structured environment of Davos, they know that I will treat them with the same respect and openness. It doesn't matter if we're surrounded by nature or inside a conference room with a Head of State—they know I'm the same person in both places. This consistency helps build trust, showing people that I value them for who they are, not just for their roles or titles.

Creating trust in a diverse environment isn't just about what we say; it's about what we do. It's about being consistent, respectful, and genuinely interested in understanding others. When people see that you are willing to listen and learn from them, they are more likely to trust you. This is especially important in settings where cultural differences might create barriers. By openly engaging with these differences, we create an atmosphere where trust can grow, even in the most complex situations.

Trust is fragile, and there are times when it can be broken. When that happens, I believe in confronting the issue directly. The first step is to acknowledge what went wrong. Transparency is crucial. People must know their concerns are heard and taken seriously. Regardless of where the fault lies, I take responsibility and openly communicate the steps we will take to make things right.

Transparency and open communication are the foundation upon which trust is built and maintained within any community. Without these, misunderstandings can quickly arise, leading to feelings of exclusion, suspicion, and even a complete breakdown in trust. In every leadership role I've taken, I've prioritized clear communication, keeping everyone informed about decisions, challenges, and the broader vision we're working toward. When people understand the reasoning behind decisions and have access to information, they feel more connected to the process, confident in their leaders, and committed to the collective mission. Sometimes I was successful, and sometimes I wasn't. It's important to also acknowledge that the route to success as a leader is never linear.

Maintaining transparency is not just about sharing successes; it's equally about being honest when things don't go as planned. I've learned that being open during difficult moments truly builds trust. It shows that, as a leader, you are celebrating the highs and guiding the community through the lows. By openly addressing challenges and setting clear steps for how we plan to overcome them, people feel reassured, and trust grows more robust.

One effective way to ensure transparency is through governance structures. Boards, advisory committees, or Community Champions play a crucial role in amplifying trust and ensuring communication is not just top-down. For example, we implemented a structure in the Global Shapers Community where key stakeholders—Advisory Council members or Community Champions—served as bridges between leadership and community members. This setup allowed communication to flow freely, especially not to be lost in translation and made community members feel informed and represented in decision-making processes. Trust cannot rest on one person's shoulders; it must be built and reinforced collectively.

During times of crisis or uncertainty, transparency becomes even more critical. I remember specific moments when the community faced challenges and looked to leadership for guidance and reassurance. In those times, I didn't just offer immediate solutions. I first ensured everyone knew we were in it together for the long haul. Addressing the immediate concerns was just the beginning—I made a point of keeping the conversation going. After explaining the situation, I would arrange a follow-up meeting or send out detailed communications such as newsletters or posts in our digital platform, so everyone understood this process was ongoing. This kind of continuous communication is essential to maintaining trust—it shows that transparency is not a one-time gesture but a steady commitment to openness.

Integrating transparent conversations into larger gatherings like summits can have an incredibly profound effect on the community. It's more than just providing updates; it's about fostering an environment where everyone feels seen, heard, and involved in the decision-making process. When you openly address tough topics—whether they're about a problematic situation or explaining the rationale behind decisions—you create a sense of collective ownership. People begin to understand that their voices truly matter and that their concerns are acknowledged, not brushed aside.

This openness nurtures trust and strengthens the bond within the community. It helps people feel like they're part of something larger, where transparency and honesty are at the core. I'll never forget the moment during a Global Shapers summit when I addressed the issue of sexual harassment in my opening plenary. I stood before the entire community and said that no community, including ours, is immune to this issue. I emphasized that just because we hadn't faced it yet didn't mean it wouldn't happen. I wanted everyone to know that we had put in place strong mechanisms, like a third-party hotline, to ensure that if anyone ever experienced harassment, they had a safe space to report it.

The reaction was powerful. Many were visibly moved and approached me afterwards to express their gratitude. Some were surprised that I had the courage to openly discuss such a sensitive topic on that platform. But to me, and to the team, it was necessary. Speaking openly about these issues showed that our community was committed to safeguarding everyone, no matter how uncomfortable. It wasn't just about words but about action, transparency, and building trust.

Establishing trust within a community creates a ripple effect that enhances collaboration, innovation, and resilience. Trust empowers individuals to take risks, share ideas, and engage fully because they know they have the support of their peers. This shared confidence leads to a stronger, more connected community that can face challenges together. The impact of trust extends beyond immediate relationships; it influences the overall growth and health of the community, allowing it to take on bigger and more ambitious goals.

Trust was the critical foundation for the significant growth and resilience of the Global Shapers Community. When I assumed the responsibility of leading this dynamic global network, the challenge wasn't just managing its existing structure but nurturing its growth in size and impact. The community's ability to flourish, expanding into over 500 cities worldwide, rested entirely on trust.

This trust didn't come from the top down; it was cultivated from within. Shapers knew, without hesitation, that they could rely on one another, no matter the distance or differences in backgrounds. It wasn't just about collaboration—it was about a deep belief in the community's integrity, commitment, and shared vision. This foundation of trust allowed for extraordinary achievements, even in the face of global challenges.

Trust fueled the community's growth and strengthened its capacity for influence. It allowed the Shapers to extend their initiatives beyond local impact and into the global arena, working together to shape conversations and drive action on issues that affected millions. One poignant example of this came during the beginning of the COVID-19 pandemic. When the virus first emerged in China, a dangerous narrative spread, labeling it as the "Chinese virus." This rhetoric fueled racism, division, and fear in many parts of the world. In response, Chinese Shapers launched a global media campaign to counter this harmful narrative, emphasizing unity over division. This swift mobilization was only possible because of the pre-existing trust within the community, empowering Shapers from all over the world to collaborate quickly and effectively to spread the campaign across the globe.

Similarly, when Ebola devastated parts of West Africa, Shapers from Guinea to Liberia, Sierra Leone, Mali, Senegal, and Nigeria launched projects to respond, coordinating efforts to raise awareness and provide resources. Trust was again at the heart of this initiative. There was an understanding that, despite geographical distance, each hub was aligned with the same mission—to respond with care, urgency, and efficiency. This trust enabled hubs in unaffected regions to rally behind their counterparts in West Africa, offering crucial support during a difficult time.

The Community didn't expand because of rigid rules or centralized control—it grew because every member felt a deep connection to the community's core values, knowing they could count on their peers to carry the weight of their shared mission.

This trust allowed the community to operate with fluidity and cohesion that would be impossible without it. It empowered individual Shapers to step into leadership roles, confident that they had the support of a global network. It allowed hubs to take on ambitious projects, knowing they weren't alone in their efforts. It fostered a culture of shared responsibility, where every success and challenge were met with the community's collective strength.

Navigating trust issues in cross-cultural leadership requires a careful, nuanced approach. It's rooted in empathy, active listening, and a deep respect for the diverse perspectives that shape each person's worldview. Trust means different things in different cultures—what is considered trustworthy behavior in one place might not hold the same meaning elsewhere. That's why I always start by understanding the cultural norms, values, and expectations of those I work with. It's not about imposing my understanding but about creating an environment where openness and mutual understanding can thrive.

Observation plays a vital role in this process. Some might perceive me as reserved, but this is part of who I am. Before diving into more profound engagement, I observe and listen, which helps me better understand others' perspectives. This allows me to make the extra effort to connect, respect their worldview, and build trust based on genuine understanding.

A poignant example of this came after the tragic murder of George Floyd in 2020. The Global Shapers Community, like the world, was shaken. Protests erupted across the United States and spread globally, demanding accountability. Shapers from various backgrounds raised essential questions and called for change. While I deeply empathized with their concerns, many saw the demands as another way for Americans to bring their agenda to the world. Some expectations were rooted in the American context, which had issues of systemic racism. However, when considering international communities like ours, the issue will have other dimensions.

The conversations that followed were intense and often complex. Balancing the specific movements in the U.S. with the broader global perspective was challenging. I knew it was essential to listen and provide space for these discussions, just as we do for other regional dialogues. The atmosphere was highly charged, and it led us to issue the only formal statement our community has ever made—a step I personally disagreed with. However, I understood the importance of listening to what appeared to be the majority, even though, in hindsight, it was more representative of a vocal minority. For me, actions speak louder than statements, but I also recognize the significance of such a response within the context of that moment.

Throughout my time with the Global Shapers Community, I witnessed how cultural nuances and unique perspectives could shape our interactions unexpectedly. These differences, while enriching, sometimes lead to misunderstandings or even conflict if not approached thoughtfully. Cultural sensitivity proved essential, as moments like these highlighted how practices common in one part of the world could be unfamiliar—or even unfeasible—in another. Navigating these cultural distinctions required careful consideration and respect for each perspective.

An example arose during a Global Shapers Summit when a Shaper from the U.S. asked about donating unused breast milk from breastfeeding stations, a common practice in the U.S. However, we were in Switzerland, where such practices weren't typical, and legal restrictions made it unfeasible (like donating breastfed milk). This request, though well-intended, highlighted how something familiar in one culture could be unknown or even unacceptable in another.

There were also calls to include gender pronouns on name tags or recognize ancestral lands at events. While these practices were meaningful to some, they weren't widely understood or accepted in other regions. The challenge was to honor these requests, when possible, without imposing them universally and to know how to decline them without hurting sensitivities because they are well-intentioned. These experiences reinforced the importance of respecting cultural differences while staying true to the community's core values.

On that note, many Shapers have often asked me why I don't send out a New Year's Eve message to the community. My response was always rooted in the idea of inclusivity and understanding the diversity that makes our community so special. I would say, “Do I have the bandwidth to send a message on the eve of the Chinese New Year? Or the Muslim New Year? Or the Persian New Year? Or other celebrations?” The answer is no. To me, it’s either honoring each celebration to include everyone in the community or choosing not to send any message at all to avoid leaving anyone out. Of course, individual members send messages as they feel moved to do so, but as a leader, I felt it was important not to signal preference toward one culture or tradition over others. For me, it wasn’t about marking one specific day on the calendar. It was about respecting that we are a global community, each of us celebrating different traditions and marking different milestones.

This approach reflects the theme of building trust within a diverse and global community. By acknowledging and respecting the cultural differences that mold each Shaper’s experience, we create an environment of mutual respect and understanding. This reinforces the idea that leadership in a multicultural space isn’t about enforcing one standard but about embracing all the different voices, customs, and beliefs that make us who we are.

Building trust within such a diverse community involves acknowledging differences and fostering a shared sense of respect and responsibility. Just as I explained my reasoning for not sending a blanket New Year’s message to the Shapers—out of respect for the different calendars and traditions we all observe—it is also important to create inclusive environments where everyone feels valued. Trust is built when people see that every action, even small gestures, considers their unique backgrounds.

At every level, the goal is to balance individual autonomy with collective goals. The trust I work to build is rooted in mutual respect and understanding, ensuring that everyone feels heard and valued while contributing to the larger mission. Navigating trust in cross-cultural leadership isn’t about finding a one-size-fits-all solution—it’s about creating an environment where each person's unique background enriches the whole. By doing this, we create a community that thrives on diversity and is strengthened by its collective spirit.

CHAPTER 14:
EMPOWER TO TRANSFORM

"The world is changed by your example, not by your opinion."
– Paulo Coelho

A leadership philosophy should prioritize cultivating a strong sense of ownership among community members. From my experiences, I've learned that those who feel genuinely invested in a cause or project tend to contribute more and take pride in their achievements. It's about creating an environment where each person feels seen, heard, and valued—where they are not just participants but vital parts of shaping the journey and the outcome.

One of the most effective ways to encourage this sense of ownership is to involve people in decisions shaping the community's vision. This isn't just about delegating tasks; it's about ensuring each person has a stake in the future being built together. Whether choosing themes for significant events or deciding on priority projects, it's important to welcome diverse perspectives and active participation.

As a Founding Curator of the Rabat Hub, I had the chance to participate in the first Annual Curators Meeting in the summer of 2012. Together, we drafted the community's charter, line by line. This hands-on approach made us feel deeply responsible for the values we outlined. It became a tradition for every summit to revisit this process, where we'd gather to refine aspects like our values, the code of conduct, or steering committees. Through this collaborative planning, people naturally felt connected to the outcomes because they had directly shaped them.

But ownership is also about empowering people. Leadership, to me, is not about doing everything myself or controlling every detail. It's about giving people the tools, resources, and freedom to take initiative. This was especially important when working with local hub curators. We trusted them to manage their projects—whether focused on climate action, youth empowerment, or social justice—in ways that made sense for their local context. This autonomy wasn't just a task delegation; it was a way to empower them, knowing that the success of their initiatives depended on their leadership, not oversight from headquarters.

Clear communication is also crucial to building ownership. Members who understand how their contributions fit the bigger picture feel more connected to the community's mission. I remember a time during one of the Global Shapers Summits when we organized a team-building exercise to highlight this idea. We split all the Curators into 35 groups, each receiving a small section of a painting. The task seemed simple: replicate the design on a larger canvas of 1*1 meter, but what they didn't know was that their sections were part of a much bigger image. Each team focused on perfecting their piece, not realizing they were contributing to something more significant.

An hour into the exercise, we called the team leaders of each of the 35 groups. As they laid out the separate canvases, they began to see how each piece fit into a grander design. We brought all the pieces together on stage in the plenary hall, revealing a significant piece of art of the summit's logo, with the word "SHAPING" written boldly across it. The reaction was priceless—Curators were stunned to see how their efforts had come together to form a unified whole. It was a powerful reminder that every contribution matters, even when the bigger picture isn't immediately visible.

The exercise had a more profound impact than I had anticipated. During the debrief, many Curators shared their thoughts. Some spoke about their initial doubts and frustrations, worried that their small piece wouldn't be good enough. Others talked about trusting their teammates without knowing how their piece will shape. Others spoke about communication issues between them, as they didn't understand the purpose of the exercise. But in the end, the pride was unmistakable when they saw the final artwork. It was a perfect metaphor for community building—where each small effort, each contribution, creates a more significant impact than anyone could achieve alone. This experience reinforced a vital truth: leadership is not about controlling every detail but about trusting the collective power. When everyone is empowered and given the space to contribute, the outcome is always more significant than the sum of its parts, and sometimes, we aren't sure about the big picture. This shared responsibility strengthened the Curators' connection to one another and to the future of the Global Shapers Community, while also deepening their trust in the process.

One of the most significant examples of collective responsibility leading to substantial growth occurred during a pivotal moment in the Global Shapers Community. As the community expanded to hundreds of hubs worldwide, maintaining its core values and high governance standards became increasingly challenging. Some hubs had lost their sense of purpose or strayed from the community's original mission, creating an urgent need for reform.

We were faced with a critical decision: continue expanding without addressing these issues or take a difficult but necessary step to safeguard the integrity and sustainability of the community. Ultimately, we chose the latter. We decided to close over 200 hubs that no longer aligned with our values or governance standards, such as not electing a curator annually or failing to launch at least one project per year.

This decision was not made by any one individual. It emerged from a collective process that involved not only the leadership but also members of the Global Shapers team and members of governance bodies with representatives from hubs across the globe. We engaged in open, sometimes tricky, discussions, where every voice was given a microphone and a listening ear. Every member felt a sense of ownership over the future of the Global Shapers, and they recognized the importance of protecting its values for future generations.

It was a shared responsibility—everyone understood that these tough decisions had to be made to ensure long-term growth and impact. We communicated transparently about the reasons behind the closures and worked closely with the remaining hubs to provide them with the support they needed to thrive. This collective effort preserved the community's integrity and reignited the passion and commitment of hubs determined to carry the mission forward.

The outcome of this collective responsibility was a more focused, resilient community. The remaining hubs grew stronger, more unified, and dedicated to their purpose. This experience demonstrated that when a community takes responsibility together—no matter how difficult the decisions—the following growth is sustainable and deeply meaningful. It reinforced the idea that leadership is not about avoiding hard choices but about making them in a way that involves everyone and honors the shared mission.

Aligning personal interests with a community's larger goals requires careful balancing and a deep understanding of both the individual motivations of community members and the group's overarching mission. One of the first steps I take in this alignment process is to ensure that the community's goals are clearly communicated and that they resonate with its members' personal values and aspirations.

In the Global Shapers Community, I have always emphasized understanding members' personal "why"—what drives them and gives meaning to their work. When we brought members together, I prioritized listening deeply to their personal stories, their passions, and the motivations that fueled their actions. I wanted each person to feel that they were in a safe space, that they were part of an environment in which their voices were heard and valued, and even their hidden aspirations or personal agendas could be acknowledged and supported.

A crucial part of my leadership approach has always been to show my team that I was deeply invested in their roles within the community and their broader career aspirations and life ambitions. I often asked them, "What are your career objectives, and how can your current role help you achieve them?" These honest and open conversations allowed me to understand better what truly mattered to each person. Knowing their personal goals, I could align their ambitions with the larger mission of the team and the community, ensuring that their contributions felt meaningful on an individual and collective level.

It wasn't just about addressing what they wanted at the moment. It was equally important to see behind the curtains and understand what they needed to grow, even if it wasn't immediately apparent to them. For example, I've often encouraged team members to step outside their comfort zones, such as practicing public speaking, because I knew it was a critical skill for their future growth. Sometimes, I pushed them to share the stage with me, even if they weren't entirely ready or comfortable, because I recognized that taking that step would advance them to the next level. This was never about forcing them into uncomfortable situations but instead helping them see what they could and preparing them for what lay ahead.

I recall a moment that truly encapsulated the power of trust and empowerment. A young Shaper from Latin America had been invited to speak on a panel at the World Economic Forum in Davos, a dream opportunity for anyone. When she found out that she would be sharing the stage with Christine Lagarde, the former Managing Director of the International Monetary

Fund and one of her personal role models, she panicked. The weight of the moment overwhelmed her. She kept repeating, "I can't do this. I'm not ready to speak in front of someone like her."

Her nervousness was palpable, but I knew this was exactly the kind of moment where people often rise to their potential. I looked at her and said, "You may not feel ready, but I see your potential. Trust yourself. I'll be right here if you need support. You can do this." I must have repeated that reassurance a dozen times, willing her to believe in herself as much as I believed in her. With each affirmation, she started to calm down, took a deep breath, and walked onto that stage.

What happened next was nothing short of transformative. As the discussion unfolded, Christine Lagarde praised the young Shaper, highlighting her impressive insights and encouraging young people to follow her lead. The recognition from someone she so deeply admired lit a fire within her. But it didn't stop there. Later that day, she received a message from a teenage girl from Zurich who had seen the panel online. The young girl wrote, "You are my role model. And I am taking the train to Davos to meet you."

At that moment, the baton of inspiration had been passed. Watching her transform—growing in confidence with every word she spoke—was a powerful reminder of what happens when we trust people, give them opportunities to shine, and support them when they doubt themselves. It wasn't just about a panel in Davos; it was about her realizing her own potential and, in turn, inspiring the next generation.

This approach of encouraging people to step up, even when they doubt themselves, has always been at the heart of my leadership. I realized early on that when you tap into someone's personal story, their sense of purpose often becomes closely connected with the group's mission. It's like finding a key that unlocks their full potential. I made it a habit to understand what drives each person—what gets them excited, keeps them up at night thinking of new ideas, and gives them a sense of accomplishment. When people see their passions reflected in their work, they don't just contribute; they thrive.

One of the ways I encouraged this for my team, for example, was by allowing members to have a real say in what projects we took on. Instead of laying out a strict plan, I invited them. We would sit down together, discussing what mattered most to us and what goals we should focus on. I remember a time when we were working on a new climate initiative. Instead of deciding everything myself or with the team, we set up a council focused on the environment, allowing those with a deep passion for climate action to take the lead. "You know this issue best," I told them. "Show us how we can make a difference." Their excitement was palpable, and because they had a hand in shaping the project's direction, they put their hearts into making it succeed.

This way of co-creating, of shaping the future together, made all the difference. It wasn't just about completing a task or ticking off a box. It was about feeling that their voices mattered and that their ideas could shape the future of our community. When people felt that their personal passions were respected and valued, they were more motivated to give their best for themselves and the whole group. It became clear that authentic community-building happens when everyone sees their work as a reflection of their dreams.

We encouraged people to incorporate their passions into the projects they led. Some were passionate about promoting youth entrepreneurship, while others wanted to advocate for better digital access for underrepresented communities. I ensured they knew their missions could become part of the larger community goals. "Turn your passion into action," I'd say. Let's see how it can fit into the bigger picture we're building." This wasn't just a slogan but a call to take ownership of their ideas and make them real.

Creating a space where people's achievements are celebrated as part of the community's success is crucial. It's like building a bridge between individual dreams and collective goals. I ensured that it was recognized publicly when someone reached a milestone—whether a new project launch or a successful event. It wasn't about singling out one person but showing how their efforts helped move the entire group forward.

Celebrating these moments helped everyone see that personal growth and community success are deeply interconnected. When a hub's project took off, it uplifted the whole group. This created a positive cycle in which people became more engaged once they saw their successes were valued. As their engagement grew, so did the energy and momentum of the entire community. We were no longer just a collection of individuals working on separate goals; we had become a team with a shared purpose.

Aligning personal interests with community goals isn't always easy, but it's worth every effort. It's like planting a garden where each flower adds color to the landscape. By helping people connect their passions with the community's mission, we create a space where every contribution, no matter how small, makes the whole garden flourish. In the end, that's what makes a community strong—not just shared goals but shared stories, dreams, and a shared journey toward something more significant.

CHAPTER 15: THE POWER OF COLLECTIVE INTELLIGENCE

"Coming together is a beginning; keeping together is progress; working together is success."
– Henry Ford

One of the most compelling aspects of the World Economic Forum's model is its ability to unite various voices—governments, businesses, civil society, academia, and young leaders—under a single community. This multi-stakeholder model enriches discussions by combining diverse perspectives, leading to innovative solutions. It's not just about bringing people to the table; it's about unlocking the potential for collaboration between sectors. This approach is critical for tackling complex global challenges that no single sector can solve alone.

Take the Global Shapers Community, for example—a network of young leaders committed to addressing global challenges at the local level. The WEF created a platform where these young leaders can work alongside policymakers, business executives, and other influential figures. This environment allows new ideas to emerge, grounded in the real-life experiences of those directly affected by global issues. It's a system that amplifies the impact of collective actions locally and globally by ensuring that all voices are heard.

The WEF communities operate on a model that prioritizes quality over quantity. Membership in the Global Shapers or the Young Global Leaders is selective, not to create barriers but to ensure that each member is genuinely committed to the community's mission. This selective process ensures that members bring unique perspectives, maintaining a high standard for the initiatives these communities pursue. When people know they are part of a dedicated group, they feel a more substantial commitment to contribute meaningfully. This sense of belonging and shared vision helps to drive collective action forward.

Facilitation is a critical part of making these communities work well together. Gathering bright minds in one space is only the first step—effective facilitation guides the discussions, resolves conflicts, and keeps everyone focused on their goals. The WEF uses advanced facilitation methods to harness the power of collective thinking. Techniques like Agora, World Café, and workshops create an open space where participants can exchange ideas freely. These methods enable people to dive into complex issues in a setting that values each voice equally, creating shared ownership over the outcomes.

Facilitation goes beyond managing time and logistics at events like the Global Shapers Summit or Davos. It's about creating an atmosphere or a safe space where the best ideas can surface and be developed together. Facilitators play a neutral role, guiding the conversations, bridging gaps between different viewpoints, and ensuring that the group's wisdom is fully tapped into. They help establish conditions where discussions turn into actions, ensuring that the focus remains on co-creating solutions rather than just exchanging ideas.

One particular tool that enhances engagement is graphic facilitation. My first experience with this technique came at the Global Shapers Community's first Annual Curators' Meeting in 2012, and it immediately struck me as a powerful way to deepen my understanding. By turning complex discussion concepts into visual representations, graphic facilitation helps participants see the connections between ideas. A graphic facilitator sketches vital points and insights as discussions unfold, creating a visual conversation map. These visuals act as a collective memory, showing how everyone's input fits into the bigger picture. It's like watching ideas come to life on a canvas, making the discussions more engaging and accessible. It wasn't just about the art; the visuals helped people see their contributions in a new light. Participants could look at the sketches and see their ideas but also a synthesis of all discussions. It made the collaboration process more tangible, helping everyone feel like they were part of building something together.

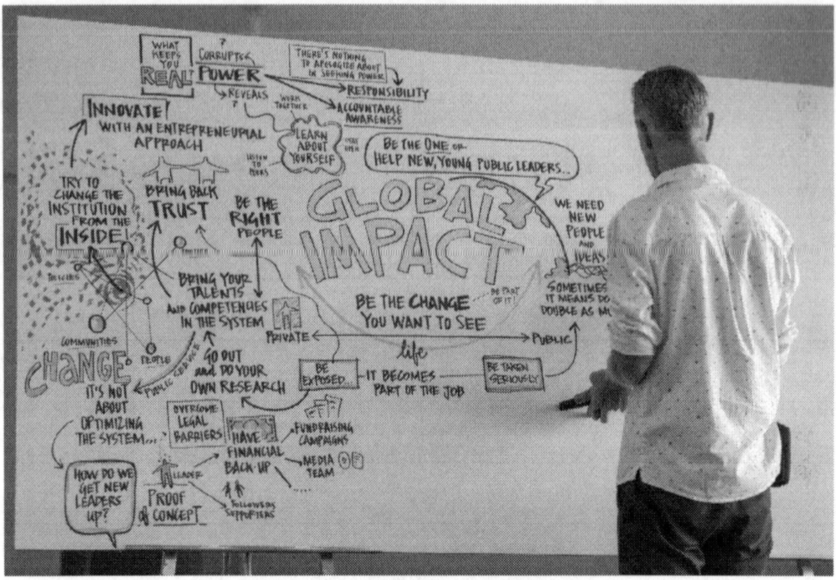

Global Shapers Summit 2019, Geneva Switzerland. Copyright by World Economic Forum / Pascal Bitz

The WEF's multi-stakeholder model thrives on dialogue and co-creation. Events like the Global Shapers Summit or the Annual Meeting in Davos aren't your typical conferences or just platforms for discussion; they are spaces where people actively work on solutions to global problems. The co-creation process is crucial; it transforms participants from passive attendees into active contributors. This model ensures that the community moves beyond conversations to achieve tangible outcomes, making a real impact on both local and global scales.

Engaging different stakeholders begins by acknowledging their unique perspectives, experiences, and motivations. It begins with identifying common ground and finding a unifying vision that resonates with everyone involved. Whether we're focusing on youth leadership, economic development, or climate action, the key is ensuring that our larger goal speaks to each participant's purpose while ensuring everyone feels they belong in the space. It's about creating an environment where stakeholders feel included, valued, and heard. The objective is not only to engage everyone in the discussion but also to encourage deep listening among all involved. This is where the role of a facilitator becomes crucial, as I've emphasized before. Actively listening, asking thoughtful questions, and drawing out the quieter voices in the room is essential to engaging diverse stakeholders. As an introvert myself, I've learned that some of the most meaningful contributions often come from those who don't speak up initially. It's our responsibility to make sure their insights are brought to the surface. Clear and open communication plays a central role in this process. Keeping everyone informed and engaged helps build trust, ensuring they feel connected to the mission and have a stake in its success.

One of the most effective strategies I use is reframing the conversation around the shared goals that brought the stakeholders together in the first place. Often, I act as a mediator, seeking compromises that allow stakeholders to achieve their critical objectives without undermining the collective purpose. One approach that has proven particularly effective is proposing phased or trial approaches. When disagreements arise about a particular initiative, it's often best to pilot different strategies on a small scale first. This allows stakeholders to see the impact before committing fully. It reduces risks and builds trust, as people see their ideas being respected and given a chance to prove their worth.

Consistent and transparent communication is essential in these situations. Regular updates, open forums, and monthly town halls help keep everyone informed and involved. I've seen how this approach prevents people from feeling blindsided by decisions. When everyone understands the reasons behind actions and sees that their voices are considered, the entire process is smoother. Focusing on the bigger picture and ensuring that all voices are valued allows us to navigate conflicting interests without losing sight of the shared goals.

Technology has become an essential tool for creating platforms for dialogue. In today's connected world, virtual meetings allow us to include people who might not be able to meet in person but have valuable insights. During the pandemic, we transitioned many global summits to online formats, ensuring that no one was excluded because of travel restrictions or health concerns. Digital tools enabled us to create virtual breakout rooms, roundtables, and even intimate one-on-one discussions, mimicking the personal touch of in-person meetings. It was incredible to see how technology allowed us to keep our global conversations alive, even when the world felt so isolated.

The future of multi-stakeholder engagement is evolving into something more dynamic, flexible, and inclusive as we face increasingly complex challenges like climate change, global health, and social inequality. Traditionally, these engagements relied on big conferences or formal meetings, but the shift now is toward continuous, real-time interaction. Digital platforms now allow governments, civil society, businesses, and individuals to keep the collaboration from anywhere in the world, breaking geographical and logistical barriers. These platforms create a space for stakeholders to meet and address issues as they arise, fostering a more responsive and adaptive way of collaborating. While technology will certainly help advance the work, I firmly believe that face-to-face interactions are essential for building trust. Technology should serve as an enabler, especially for inclusion, allowing people to contribute when barriers like visas or travel costs might otherwise prevent their participation. In the Global Shapers Community, for example, I've seen how underrepresented voices—such as those from marginalized communities, youth, and Indigenous leaders—bring unique insights but are voices that often face obstacles in joining the conversation. Inviting them to the table is not enough; their perspectives must be actively integrated into the decision-making process. I've learned through my experiences that when people feel their voices truly matter, they engage more deeply and bring forward solutions that others might miss.

This inclusivity also requires creating a safe space where everyone can speak openly. Sometimes, it can be just by reaching out to someone quiet and privately asking them if they have something they want to add or share; usually people feel empowered and can spark a whole new discussion based on their input. At some point, the Global Shapers team spanned 3 continents, with colleagues based in Beijing, New York, and Geneva. It wasn't easy for them to share and chime in as we had an existing team dynamic. We were in the same room, and we were mostly talking to each other, not to the big screen on the wall. To alter and improve our approach, we appointed one individual during our meetings who was responsible for all those joining the conversation online, ensuring we don't forget our colleagues who are not with us in the room. We kept doing this until we changed our behavior. Moments like these remind me how important it is to ensure that every voice is valued.

In the future, technology will play an even more prominent role in making these multi-stakeholder partnerships more efficient and impactful. Tools like artificial intelligence and data analytics will allow us to track project progress, helping teams make informed adjustments as needed. Having access to such insights will be a goldmine for communities, enabling them to drive projects and initiatives based on real-time data rather than assumptions. This technological integration will enhance transparency, increase accountability, and foster more dynamic collaboration, ultimately leading to better decision-making and more successful outcomes.

I see the future of multi-stakeholder engagement as deeply integrated into how we address global challenges. It's becoming a standard approach rather than an exception. These partnerships won't just be about solving specific problems—they will create systems that drive long-term, sustainable change. When diverse groups combine their skills, experiences, and resources, the solutions they create are more innovative and fairer. This power of collective action will guide us toward a more connected and resilient future.

The shift from traditional, event-based collaboration to continuous engagement means stakeholders can be more involved at every step. It's not just about gathering once a year at a big conference but about keeping the conversation going daily. This ongoing interaction allows us to address challenges as they arise, making our responses timelier and more effective. The ability to act quickly makes a huge difference in coordinating responses and supporting those who need help most.

With these changes, the role of facilitation has also evolved. It's no longer just about managing discussions in a room; it's about guiding virtual spaces where participants might be thousands of miles apart. We've had to adapt, learning to use digital tools to ensure everyone stays engaged and included. It's been a challenge, but it's also opened up new possibilities such as using interactive virtual whiteboards, allowing participants to share their ideas visually. This made it easier for everyone to follow the conversation and see how their input contributed to the bigger picture.

In this evolving landscape, I am optimistic. I've seen firsthand how bringing people together—online or in person—can create change that none of us could achieve alone. The future holds even more tremendous potential for collaboration, where each person's contribution is vital to a more considerable effort. It's a future where, through collective action, we can build a more just, sustainable, and connected world than ever before.

CHAPTER 16:
CURATING EXPERIENCES THAT MATTER

"Life is not measured by the number of breaths we take, but by the moments that take our breath away."
– Unknown

Building a strong community doesn't happen overnight. It requires planning, leadership, and governance. In the early stages, governance helps lay the foundation by defining the community's purpose, mission, and values. Governance isn't just about creating rules—it's about creating a system that reflects the community's vision and keeps everyone aligned.

In the Global Shapers Community, we worked hard to co-create our governance structures, ensuring every decision aligned with our values and mission. This intentional design process helped us establish a clear leadership, decision-making, and member participation framework. We knew that for the community to succeed, governance had to be flexible yet structured enough to support long-term growth.

As the community grew, we faced new challenges—mainly how to scale without losing our sense of identity. Governance played a crucial role here, allowing us to grow while staying connected to our original purpose. This balance between flexibility and structure ensured we could innovate and adapt while remaining true to our core values.

One way we achieved this balance was through decentralization. Each local hub had its own Curator and operated with a certain level of autonomy, while remaining connected to the broader goals of the Global Shapers Community. As we expanded to over 400 hubs globally, we introduced the role of Community Champions to support regional coordination. These champions acted as mentors to 15-25 hubs each. They helped ensure that every hub aligned with the community's mission while giving each region the freedom to address regional challenges.

Governance during this phase wasn't about control—it was about empowerment. We wanted local leaders to have the autonomy to innovate and lead, but we also needed accountability systems to keep everything on track. By introducing roles like Community Champions, we supported local leaders while ensuring the community stayed cohesive.

Governance structures also ensured that the Global Shapers Community remained inclusive and diverse. For example, the Community has gender quotas at each hub level, but also for all governing bodies. All our delegations to Forum events are 50%-50% to ensure that roles are filled by individuals who represent the diversity of the broader community. This wasn't just about checking a box—it was about creating a culture of inclusivity where all voices were heard and valued.

These governance mechanisms—whether through advisory councils, steering committees, Community Champions, or structured leadership roles—helped the Global Shapers Community scale while maintaining its core values. Prioritizing inclusivity, transparency, and accountability allowed us to create a system that empowered leaders at every level while ensuring the community stayed focused on its mission.

In addition to governance structures, engagement strategies were crucial in keeping members connected and active. We also hosted regular summits at the global (Annual Curators Meeting from 2012 to 2017, and the Global Shapers Summit from 2018 onwards) and regional levels with the SHAPE events. Members could come together, share ideas, and collaborate on projects at all levels.

Curating a community, however, goes beyond organizing events. It's about creating a strategic foundation that binds people, values, and purpose. Every aspect of a community event must be anchored in the broader mission and desired long-term impact of the community. From my experience at the World Economic Forum, I learned that successful community events don't happen in isolation; they're always part of a bigger story.

At the core of this work is understanding the community's purpose. Why does the community exist? What does it aim to achieve? Purpose is the guiding force behind every group decision, interaction, and action. In the Global Shapers Community, we aimed to empower young leaders to make a local impact while contributing to global change. Similarly, the YGL Community focused on bringing leaders together to share ideas, shape policies, and inspire collective action for societal good.

However, understanding the community's system is just as important. Communities aren't just groups of individuals; they include multiple stakeholders who both influence and are influenced by the group's activities. It's about identifying key players—internal members or external partners—and understanding their dynamics. Managing these relationships ensures the community stays aligned with its purpose and remains functional.

When planning community events, ensuring they're not standalone occurrences is essential. Events should be woven into the community's larger engagement plan. Each event should act as a steppingstone or a continuation of the community's journey. This way, the event becomes more than just a moment—it becomes a significant part of building lasting relationships and driving collective action. Whether a regional

SHAPE event or a global leadership summit, the event should always be tied to the community's long-term goals.

To foster deep connections and a sense of shared ownership, every participant should feel like they play a role in shaping the community. This creates a feeling of belonging and shared responsibility, vital for the community's sustainability and long-term impact.

Curating meaningful community events requires going beyond logistical details to focus on experience design. The ReCode Cube Model, developed by TheValueWeb, is a robust framework for navigating the complexity of communities and influencing systems for change. This model consists of six key dimensions: Purpose, Players, Structure, Process, Facilitation, and Sharing—all crucial to building impactful communities and hosting successful events.

I had the opportunity to be trained in this model by TheValueWeb and apply it in several significant events. Through these experiences, I saw firsthand how the ReCode Cube Model helped design environments where collaboration flourished. It enables the creation of collaborative spaces that extend beyond the event itself and ripple out to influence larger systems and networks. The model's beauty is that it evolves continuously, making it especially effective for designing in-person, hybrid, or virtual meetings.

The first and most important dimension of the ReCode Cube Model is purpose. Purpose is the foundation of everything. It determines an event's direction, goals, and impact. Events risk becoming disconnected from the community's broader strategy without a clear purpose. Before planning any gathering, it's essential to ask: "Why are we doing this? What change do we want to make? What outcomes do we want to achieve?"

Purpose needs to be tightly connected to the community's mission. In the Global Shapers Community and the YGL Community, the purpose was always about empowering young leaders and driving positive change, both locally and globally. Every event had to align with this purpose, so participants knew what they were working toward.

Once the purpose is set, the next step is identifying the players. These people and stakeholders need to be involved to make the event successful. A community comprises diverse individuals with various skills, experiences, and perspectives. Bringing the right mix of people together is essential. One critical lesson from using the ReCode Cube Model and MGTaylor's approaches was the importance of diversity in selecting players.

For example, when planning Global Shapers summits, we always included a wide range of voices—whether they were youth leaders, external partners, or policymakers. Diversity wasn't just about ensuring representation across race, gender, or geography; it also included diversity of thought, experiences, and skills. As the ReCode Cube Model teaches, the right mix of people must be chosen for their expertise and how they can collectively contribute to the community's purpose.

The careful selection of participants ensures that the event benefits from rich discussions and meaningful collaboration. I've seen firsthand how bringing together people from different backgrounds can lead to unexpected insights, innovation, and more substantial outcomes. The diversity of players often creates synergies that make the event more impactful.

With the players in place, the next step in the ReCode Cube Model is establishing the structure. This involves creating the framework for how the event will unfold, from the agenda to the roles and responsibilities of everyone involved. The structure ensures that the event flows smoothly and that participants clearly understand their roles.

Then comes the process, which is how the event will be conducted. The process is all about creating opportunities for engagement and collaboration. Every event step must be designed to encourage meaningful interaction between participants. In Global Shapers events, we used processes like breakout sessions, workshops, and open discussions to ensure that everyone's voice was heard. We also left moments for emergence. I always loved to tell the team, "How can we engineer serendipity?" What moment can we create for the right minds to meet, collaborate, and create a positive impact?

Facilitation is the next dimension. It's about guiding the event and creating an environment where people feel comfortable sharing ideas and collaborating. A good facilitator knows how to balance the conversation, ensure that all voices are heard, and keep the event focused on its purpose. Facilitation here is very different from moderation. Whereas moderation tends to control the flow of conversation and stick to predetermined outcomes, facilitation is about unlocking the collective intelligence of the group. It's about creating the space for ideas to emerge, fostering open dialogue, and encouraging participants to take ownership of the outcomes. The facilitator serves more as a guide, ensuring that the energy of the group remains aligned with the event's goals, while allowing organic collaboration to take root. It's not about directing the conversation but rather nurturing the dynamic exchanges and keeping the group aligned with the bigger picture. A skilled facilitator also knows when to step back and let the group self-organize, knowing that the magic often happens when people feel empowered to lead from within.

In many events I've curated, we focused on ensuring that participants walked away with new knowledge and relationships. One way we did this was by prioritizing informal interactions. We built plenty of time for informal networking—over meals, during breaks, and in social settings—where participants could connect personally—these casual moments often led to deeper, more meaningful relationships.

I overheard two participants discussing their projects during a coffee break at one event. "It's funny," one said, "I came here to learn about leadership, but the best part has been meeting people like you." This comment reminded me of how powerful these informal moments can be. While the structured sessions are essential, it's often the spontaneous conversations that create the most vital and memorable connections.

However, structure is essential to making these events work. Without a well-organized structure, even the best ideas can lose their impact. Structure shapes the timeline, interaction spaces, and touchpoints for engagement. While planning these events, we learned that the structure had to be flexible, allowing unexpected but essential moments to emerge.

For example, during one of the Global Shapers Summit and while I was ringing the traditional Swiss Davos bell to signal it's time to return to the plenary, I noticed a small group of participants gathering on a sofa, engaging in an impromptu debate. I overheard one of them saying, "This moment feels like we're getting somewhere." They connected on a deeper level, sharing ideas that sparked new possibilities. Instead of steering them back to the schedule, we allowed the conversation to flow, adjusting the structure to let these organic connections grow. While structure is important, leaving room for flexibility is even more essential.

We always designed our events to have breakout discussions and moments of reflection where participants could actively engage and contribute their ideas. The structure wasn't just about logistics; it was about creating meaningful spaces where participants could interact and make lasting connections.

Next comes the process—the steps or activities participants go through during the event. The process moves people from passive listening to active participation, from just talking about ideas to taking action. In the Global Shapers Community and the Young Global Leaders events, I saw how a well-thought-out process could empower participants to co-create solutions.

For instance, we often organize group problem-solving sessions at Global Shapers Summits. Participants were grouped into small teams and tasked with finding solutions to challenges. This collaborative approach fostered engagement and ensured that the event had tangible outcomes.

Another important aspect of our events was the idea of system change. We approached communities not as isolated groups but as interconnected systems. Each member brings a unique perspective, and events should create opportunities for these voices to interact and co-create solutions. This is where the system change approach from MGTaylor's methodology became crucial. It taught us to see the community as an interconnected web of relationships, each contributing to a more extensive system.

CHAPTER 17: **CURATING EVENTS: BEHIND THE SCENES**

"An event is not over until everyone is tired of talking about it."
– Mason Cooley

Organizing a community event is as much about logistics as it is about the human element. It's easy to think that the heart of any gathering lies only in the connections and experiences shared. But logistics is the backbone, the part that holds everything together. From selecting the right venue to keeping participants informed, logistics shape the entire experience. Even the best-planned discussions or workshops can falter if logistical issues disrupt the flow. This is why I've learned to prioritize meticulous planning and strong communication at every step. As Dwight D. Eisenhower said, "Plans are nothing; planning is everything."

Preparation is where it all begins. Drawing from the ReCode Cube Model explained in the last chapter, I've come to recognize that while every aspect of an event must be planned with precision, it must also be flexible enough to adapt to unexpected changes. The choice of venue, for instance, has to meet the event's needs. Each space should allow for large gatherings and smaller discussions, and it must offer room for people to connect informally. Timing, too, requires a careful balance. We need content-heavy sessions and moments for rest, reflection, and spontaneous conversations that give attendees space to process and connect.

One principle I'll always emphasize is overcommunication. Early on, I realized how crucial it is to keep participants informed before the event begins. Clear, consistent communication helps participants feel prepared and reduces any anxiety that may exist around the event. The last thing anyone should worry about is where they must be or how to navigate the schedule. This kind of clarity lets them focus entirely on the event itself.

For instance, days before an event, we'd ensure every participant received all the necessary details—location, schedule, transportation options, and even helpful reminders about what to bring. And that preparation makes a massive difference in the overall experience.

Once the event is underway, communication continues to play a central role. Real-time updates via an event app or a messaging platform allow everyone to stay in sync. Participants should know immediately if there's a last-minute schedule change or an additional networking opportunity. This creates a sense of flow, letting them know that every aspect of their experience is carefully managed. Nightly messages are highly recommended and should include updates from the day and a synthesis of the highlights of the next one. This continuous dialogue reassures everyone that they're well-informed and actively part of the event's rhythm.

When planning an event, I rely heavily on a practical checklist to ensure that every detail is covered. It's a comprehensive guide that I update and refer to regularly. Here's a sample of how I approach the planning process:

Pre-Event Planning

- Start by holding a co-creation meeting with stakeholders to define the event's goals, objectives, theme, and purpose.

- Use a chart to map out tasks and deadlines, assigning team members to each role.
- Lock in the event date and location as early as possible.
- Develop a thorough budget that covers everything. In my experience, the biggest budget items are the venue costs, meals, transportation, and accommodation.

Building the Agenda

- Organize discussions with stakeholders to co-create an agenda. We always include a mix of plenary sessions, breakout discussions, and informal networking slots. Avoid one-way lecturing—it's boring and passé!
- Ensure time is allocated for reflection and organic interactions. These less structured moments often become the most meaningful. Always leave time for serendipity.
- Double-check that every part of the agenda aligns with the event's goals and the community's objectives.
- Always ensure that the big picture of the agenda has a flow and a thread, and that participants are taken on a journey or experience throughout the event.

Another critical component of planning is defining team roles and responsibilities. Each team member has a specific role, which is essential to understand. Here's a breakdown:

- **Program Curator:** Responsible for building the big picture and coordinating content. Work also with security and safety, protocol if any, and partners.
- **Participant Liaison:** Manages communication with participants, from registration and invitations to daily updates and feedback surveys. Visa support might fall on this role!
- **Logistics Coordinator:** Looks after transportation, accommodation, meals, and AV support.

- **Sustainability Lead:** Ensures eco-friendly practices like waste reduction and low energy use.
- **Technology Coordinator:** Manages virtual event components, presentations, streaming, and digital platforms.
- **Communication Lead:** Works with designers on branding, drafts all communication materials, and oversees social media, sponsorships, and traditional media.

Effective communication extends to the team itself. It's crucial to schedule regular (weekly, in our case) check-ins to ensure everyone is clear on their tasks. Setting up a real-time communication platform like Slack, Teams, or WhatsApp lets the team stay connected during the event and helps them respond to any issues in real time.

I've found that planning is critical to participant engagement. Invitations are sent out well ahead of time, as well as follow-up confirmations. We also provide detailed logistical information, including venue addresses, transportation details, dietary needs, and any available financial aid. A solid communication plan for sending reminders and updates keeps the event top-of-mind for everyone involved.

As the event day arrives, logistical execution becomes the focus. This includes:

- **Venue & Accommodation:** Set up a few days before the event, arrange transportation, accommodations, and coordinate catering.
- **Technology & AV:** Test all AV equipment, ensure reliable internet access, and have tech support on standby. Consider providing charging stations for participants.
- **Transportation & Meals:** Manage participant transportation, plan meals, and address dietary needs (surveys are sent ahead of time for vegetarians, vegans, and those with allergies). Have water fountains everywhere and ask partic-

ipants to bring their own water bottle for reuse or provide them as goodies.

- **Photography & Documentation:** Assign a photographer and set up plans to document the event with photos and videos. Have a plan to share these every day, or it will be too late for them to share on their social media accounts.
- **Goodies & Prints:** Ordering eco-friendly materials like programs, printouts for participants, and water bottles.

One area that is always important to prioritize is sustainability. Waste reduction should be a core focus, with recycling stations set up to ensure minimal waste. Minimize single-use plastics and reduce paper use by relying on digital communication whenever possible. Encouraging public transportation or car/bus-sharing among participants is another practice that needs to be implemented to lessen the event's environmental impact. Managing food waste is equally important. Careful planning helps order the right amount of food to ensure there is no food waste.

While curating events, I rely on tools like the Gantt chart or Strawdogs to keep all these logistics in check. This chart serves as a visual roadmap for the entire event timeline, helping track every task, ensuring nothing falls through the cracks. Many templates can be found online to help you streamline the organization process. It answers vital questions like: What tasks need to be completed? Who's responsible for each item? Where are we in the timeline?

With the Gantt chart, I can see every step, from initial planning to post-event wrap-up, at a single glance. The chart becomes a daily guide, showing what's already been done and what still needs attention, which keeps the entire process organized. Strawdogs are detailed, organized by the minute with information on what needs to be done and by whom. It helps with lighting, presentation slides, when someone needs to be on stage, or when handouts need to be distributed.

When setting up the Gantt chart for an event, it's important to break down each phase. The pre-event planning phase includes everything from booking venues to securing vendors. Then, content curation—planning the agenda, confirming speakers, and ensuring topics align with the event's theme. Logistics and tech come next, with dates for confirming transportation, audiovisual equipment, and sustainability practices. Finally, there's participant engagement, where timelines are set for sending invitations, reminders, and post-event feedback requests.

However, logistics also rely heavily on clear communication within the team. Assigning roles isn't enough; each team member must understand their responsibilities and how their work fits the event's broader goals. Regular check-ins, open discussions, and clear communication channels ensure everyone is aligned. During the event, each team member's role becomes even more critical. The programme curator, for instance, keeps sessions on schedule and ensures facilitators are ready. The participant liaison handles participant's needs, while the logistics coordinator oversees transportation, meals, and audiovisual setups. The technology coordinator ensures all digital tools run smoothly, without interruptions. These clear roles and communication lines create a cohesive workflow, minimizing miscommunication and delays.

Every aspect of logistics impacts the participant experience. From the venue layout to the timing of sessions and the arrangement of networking spaces, logistics influence how participants engage with the event and each other. A well-timed break allows for casual conversations that might spark new ideas, while thoughtful scheduling ensures that sessions are engaging without exhausting attendees. Venue setup also matters; comfortable seating, easily accessible areas, and a warm atmosphere encourage active engagement. Every detail speaks!

One of the most subtle yet powerful lessons I absorbed during my time at the World Economic Forum was the impact of presence and pace in high-stakes environments. I learned that it's essential to avoid rushing from one place to another or appearing hurried. Moving calmly, and not running, for example, even under pressure, sends a powerful, stabilizing signal to everyone around you. This seemingly small detail—the way we carry ourselves physically—can create an atmosphere of reassurance or, conversely, of silent chaos. When we rush, even if unintentionally, we broadcast an unconscious message that something is off, which, in turn, can spark anxiety and doubt in those around us.

It's as though people, on a primal level, sense disruption and instability when they see someone in authority racing. That hurried energy communicates, "There's a problem," even if nothing has gone wrong. This awareness is particularly crucial when working in high-pressure environments where participants may already feel the weight of important conversations or decisions. By moving with a calm, assured pace, I learned to embody stability, sending an implicit message: "Everything is under control; you're in a safe space."

In time, I realized this practice was less about me and more about fostering a collective sense of calm and focus. I've seen firsthand how a calm, unhurried presence can bring out the best in people, allowing them to engage more deeply, feel more secure, and focus on what truly matters. The lesson taught me that true leadership often lies not in grand gestures but in the quiet, consistent presence that reassures others, letting them know that even in the busiest moments, all is well.

The above, as well as logistics in general, should support a human-centered event design, ensuring participants feel comfortable, engaged, and ready to contribute. This approach ensures that the event not only meets its goals but also resonates with participants on a personal level, creating a memorable and impactful experience.

But the true success of any event extends far beyond the closing session. In fact, what happens after the event is often just as important as the event itself. Every gathering should catalyze long-term engagement, deepen connections, and encourage continued participant collaboration.

One of the first steps in post-event engagement is turning event insights into ongoing conversations. Shortly after the event, sending out a feedback survey to all participants is important. This is to gauge their experience and let them share what they've learned and how they'd like to stay engaged. The survey's open-ended questions provide valuable insights, allowing participants' voices to be heard. Feedback also shows that participant's opinions are valued and there is a commitment to improving future events.

A post-event report summarizing the outcomes, critical discussions, and actionable insights is seen as a roadmap and is something participants always appreciate. This report should be shared with all attendees, allowing them to reflect on their learning. Providing a tangible document with video recordings, photos, and resources from the event keeps the conversation alive. It allows participants to revisit important community moments and extends the event's impact beyond its duration. In my experience, sending the report should not exceed a few days—one week at max—or it will lose its momentum. Thus, it is important to have this task scheduled way before the event, with a skeleton of the report ready to be updated with content and photos.

Connecting participants is another crucial step. Ensuring that people can stay in touch after the event reinforces the relationships they've built. If you don't have an app with all participants' contact information, it's recommended that you send out a follow-up email with a participant directory (for those who consented) or set up a new communication platform, like Slack or WhatsApp, where they can continue discussions.

Long-term engagement also means creating opportunities for continuous collaboration. Participants should always feel there are ways to stay involved, build on the work they started together, and bring new ideas to the projects at hand. Often, this means forming smaller working groups, planning follow-up meetings, or creating shared online spaces where people can work on projects that stem from the event's discussions. If a particular topic or challenge resonates strongly, invite participants to co-create solutions or build something meaningful together. This keeps the energy alive, and in doing so, creates a sense of shared purpose that stretches beyond the community event's final moments.

Another essential component of effective follow-up is creating opportunities for networking and relationship building. Events are often just the beginning of new relationships, and post-event engagement allows these connections to deepen. Rather than letting these relationships fade, create ways for participants to keep in touch, like periodic virtual meet ups or smaller gatherings. Treat networking as a continuous process requiring attention and nurturing, like any relationship.

Keeping communication flowing is also vital for long-term engagement. Regular updates, newsletters, or thoughtful check-ins help participants feel connected to the community's journey. Share relevant articles written by participants on their thoughts about the topics discussed, updates on projects, or developments related to themes discussed at the event. Each communication aims to bring value rather than simply reminding them of the event.

Another way to sustain engagement is by offering participants leadership opportunities within the community. People stay connected when they feel they have a role in shaping the community's future. Providing chances to lead projects, organize discussions, or mentor newer participants brings a sense of responsibility and investment. As they take on these roles, participants start seeing the community as something they help build, not just something they attend.

Emphasize the importance of reflection and integration after each event. The goal is not just for participants to absorb information but to reflect on how they can apply what they've learned. Post-event workshops, action challenges, or smaller reflection groups give them the space to connect event insights with their daily lives and professional paths. This reflection ensures the event has a lasting impact.

Maintaining a shared sense of purpose is crucial to sustaining this momentum. A community thrives when united around a common vision. While enthusiasm can easily wane once an event concludes, regular reminders of the core goals and values keep everyone aligned with the broader mission. Framing each event within this larger purpose and reinforcing it through ongoing post-event engagement strengthens the community's collective journey.

Beyond individual engagement, work to leverage each event for future community growth. Post-event strategies highlight the event's impact, using it as a foundation for upcoming initiatives. Sharing stories or testimonials from participants is one way we build excitement for future events, showcasing how these gatherings have made a difference. Each story shared adds credibility and highlights the real-world impact of what the community accomplishes together.

Publicizing outcomes is equally important. After each event, highlight any new initiatives launched, partnerships formed, or projects created, emphasizing that the event's influence stretches far beyond the few days it took place. Participants who see tangible results feel encouraged to remain active, knowing their contributions lead to lasting change. Seeing these outcomes reminds everyone that their involvement has a meaningful impact.

Post-event engagement is also an ideal time for recruitment and outreach. When participants leave an event feeling inspired, they often become ambassadors, sharing their experiences with others and inviting new members into the fold. By providing clear pathways for newcomers to join and engage in post-event initiatives, you can expand the community's reach. This strengthens the network and brings fresh ideas and perspectives that keep the community dynamic.

The ultimate goal of any well-organized event is to turn a decisive moment into sustained momentum. The aim to ensure that the relationships, ideas, and energy generated during the event live on long after the final session ends. Thoughtful follow-up, consistent communication, and clear collaboration opportunities build a bridge from each event to the next. In this way, the impact of a single event extends far beyond its original scope, creating a community that grows stronger, more resilient, and more interconnected over time.

PART 4:

FUTURE TRENDS IN COMMUNITY LEADERSHIP

CHAPTER 18: LEADING LOCALLY, CONNECTING GLOBALLY: EVOLVING GOVERNANCE

"The sun does not forget a village just because it is small."
– African Proverb

The world is changing fast, and as communities grow, so must the structures that guide them. The old ways, with decisions made by a central authority far removed from local realities, just don't work either. Communities driven by the passion and commitment of volunteers—especially younger generations—need flexibility, inclusivity, and responsiveness. And so, a new model emerges, one that respects both the central values and the unique local needs.

One remarkable thing about the shift in community governance is how it gives power back to those closest to the issues. A central philosophy still guides everything, but there's room for local leaders to take charge. They're the ones who know what their communities need, after all. The Global Shapers Community serves as a strong example of this approach. Here, each local hub can create initiatives that align with its community's specific context while staying true to the overarching values set by the headquarters. This balance is critical—it's a blend of independence and connection, allowing local leaders to shape projects that matter most to their people but within a framework that keeps everyone aligned with a shared purpose.

Of course, there are challenges with this kind of autonomy. With freedom comes the responsibility to stay accountable, to ensure that every part of the community upholds its integrity. This is where servant leadership comes in. Instead of dictating from afar, central leadership offers resources, guidance, and a solid value framework on which local hubs can depend. In this setup, the HQ is not a distant, untouchable entity but a collaborative force. It serves as the central point where everyone can connect, share experiences, and strengthen the bond that unites the community, even with each hub operating with a degree of independence.

One of the recurring issues in global community governance is the influence of Western perspectives. Often, the central offices of these communities, organizations, or even the UN are located in Western countries, which can unintentionally lead to a worldview that doesn't always align with the realities faced in other regions. There's good intentions behind the central values and strategies, but these don't always resonate in places with very different cultural, social, and political landscapes. Recognizing this, communities are increasingly moving toward a truly global structure, not just in name but in practice. By setting up multiple offices across various regions, there's a genuine effort to bring in diverse voices and make decisions that reflect a broader range of experiences and viewpoints.

The idea of multiple offices isn't just symbolic. It allows leaders in different regions to have a real say in the community's direction. Decisions no longer need to be filtered through a single office; instead, they reflect insights from different geographies. This structure helps prevent any single narrative from dominating and allows for a leadership style that's more inclusive of the many unique experiences within the community. Having these multiple centers means that decisions can be grounded in the local realities of each region, which keeps the community's overall mission relevant and adaptable. I've also observed that many organizations and communities attempt to "check the box" on diversity by hiring individuals from the Global South for their Western offices. However, these hires are often individuals who have been educated in Western institutions, reflecting a Western perspective rather than truly diverse viewpoints. I remember a prominent headhunting firm, tasked with identifying high-achieving leaders, excluding candidates who had only gone through the local education systems in the Global South. This decision was made under the assumption—after due diligence—that these individuals might pose a "risk." Unless we are genuinely committed to meaningful diversity that values unique backgrounds and local perspectives, this superficial approach will continue to prevail. True diversity requires embracing the rich, unique insights that come from varied educational, cultural, and regional experiences, rather than filtering talent through a Westernized lens.

When I think about diversity in governance or structure, I realize it's not just about geographical reach. It's about pulling in different backgrounds, ethnicities, religions, races, and social perspectives, giving each one a place in decision-making. Historically, voices from the Global South have been overlooked or instructed rather than genuinely included, especially in global spaces where key decisions are made. The world is moving forward, though, slowly realizing that leadership should reflect all voices, not just a few. There's a shift happening where no one's origin should affect their ability to have a voice in shaping their community. I often think of the labels we use—how someone from a Western country moving south is called an "expat," while someone from the Global South moving to the West is seen as a "migrant." These small yet powerful distinctions remind me of the need for a governance model that is genuinely inclusive and aware of these disparities.

Building a community that's truly global requires commitment and openness to change. The decision to establish a network of regional offices instead of centralizing everything in one location is a strong step toward this goal. It's a statement that the community values diversity not just in words but in actions. This structure allows each member or local entity to retain its cultural identity, to build projects that resonate with its members, while still connecting with the broader mission. It's a flexible model that adapts to the needs of local leaders and ensures that every region's voice is heard. In navigating this structure, a central element remains the community's Impact Model or Theory of Change. The model brings everyone together with clear goals and a shared understanding of how change happens. Each member or local entity might operate independently, but they're all working within this same framework, guided by core principles and driven by the desire to make a positive difference. For instance, one hub might focus on education initiatives while another takes on environmental issues, yet both are aligned under the same vision. The Impact Model keeps everyone on course, showing how individual projects feed into a bigger picture, and it provides measurable outcomes to see exactly how each effort contributes to the overall mission.

The Theory of Change is another crucial piece of this governance puzzle. It serves as a roadmap, detailing how each action taken within the community—no matter how small—leads toward a greater impact. With every step, from planning to execution, there's a clear path laid out that links inputs, activities, and outcomes. It's inspiring to see how each component connects. This theory isn't just an abstract concept but a practical guide that helps focus the resources and energies toward meaningful change.

These governance principles give the community its resilience and adaptability. In a world tangled with complex, interconnected challenges, the need for balance between local autonomy and global unity is more crucial than ever. This approach to governance is both empowering and humbling. It's a trust given to local leaders, recognizing their understanding and dedication to their communities. But at the same time, it's a reminder that unity, a shared purpose, is what holds everything together. This model doesn't just lead a community; it creates a solid foundation for growth, allowing everyone to evolve in their unique way while staying true to the larger mission. It's a fine balance, a dance between independence and interdependence, and I believe this balance is what will sustain the community's strength for years to come.

Accountability and transparency are also crucial pillars of this evolving governance. With decentralization, it becomes even more important to have structures that ensure local leaders and hubs align with the community's core values. Autonomy could lead to inconsistency or a disconnect from the community's mission without a solid foundation for accountability. Diverse boards, advisory councils, and governance committees provide checks and balances. These structures keep decision-making fair, and they ensure that choices reflect a broader range of perspectives. I think of an advisory board as a mosaic of different views that challenge each other and offer insights, grounding the leadership in fairness and keeping the community on track.

Embracing technology has been another game-changer in creating accountability and participation across the board. Digital tools make it possible to report transparently, provide real-time feedback, and include voices that might otherwise be left out due to distance or limited resources. As community governance continues to grow, these tech advancements play an essential role. Now, members from any corner of the world can raise their voice, ask questions, and influence the community's path. The potential here is huge—it means we can genuinely include everyone, regardless of where they are.

Ultimately, I see the future of community governance resting on a delicate balance between local autonomy and central oversight. There's a need to empower diverse leaders, giving them ownership and letting them bring their unique strengths to the table. Yet, there's an equally strong need to maintain the values and accountability that bind the community together.

I see it as a structure that's flexible enough to adapt to local needs but solid enough to uphold the principles that make this community what it is.

As the world becomes more interconnected, I'm certain that these trends in governance will shape how communities function, ensuring that they stay inclusive, responsive, and capable of leaving a lasting impact. With each new change, we're building a structure that isn't just about making decisions—it's about supporting a vision for the future, a vision that includes everyone and responds to the world we're living in. This approach gives me hope, knowing that we're creating something that not only adapts to the present but builds a foundation for the future.

CHAPTER 19: THE HUMAN ELEMENT IN THE ARTIFICIAL INTELLIGENCE AGE

"The more we elaborate our means of communication, the less we communicate."
– J.B. Priestley

As we stand on the brink of what we call the Fourth Industrial Revolution, I can feel the energy, excitement, and challenges. Technology has embedded itself into nearly every part of our lives, from how we work and learn to how we connect. Artificial intelligence, machine learning, and other new technologies have taken over tasks once performed by people, making our lives faster and more efficient. But amid all this change, one question remains: How do we hold on to what makes us human in this increasingly digital world?

Leadership today feels different. It's no longer just about making decisions or driving initiatives forward; it's about striking a delicate balance. On the one hand, technology enables us to do incredible things and push boundaries we couldn't have imagined. But on the other, there's a real need to keep empathy, trust, and genuine connection at the heart of our interactions. As I think about this, it hits me that the responsibility to find that balance doesn't just rest with technology developers or policymakers. It rests with each of us, especially those leading communities. The task is not just about being efficient but about being present.

In one of the recent World Economic Forum reports on the Future of Jobs, a powerful insight was shared: 60% of children in primary school today will end up working in jobs that don't even exist yet. The world is shifting almost dizzily, and that statistic sits heavily with me. For these children—and everyone, really—the future won't just demand new skills; it will require an entirely new mindset. The digital world offers extraordinary tools and resources, but without the human touch, it feels empty.

The transformation is happening whether we're ready or not. Technology isn't slowing down, and rather than resisting, I think more about embracing it wisely. There's a need to shift perspectives, to stop seeing technology as something that might overshadow human connection and instead recognize it as something that can amplify it. As I consider this, I wonder about the next generation. I think of my role in setting an example and helping build a world where technology and humanity coexist and support each other. It's a complex task, but I'm learning that the most valuable things often come with some complexity.

Even as I work to embrace this new digital era, the human element keeps pulling me back to the center of everything. Communities, after all, are built on relationships, trust, and a sense of belonging—things that no app or algorithm can fully replicate. One incident comes to mind that brought this reality home. It was during the virtual Global Shapers Summit that one of our most dedicated hubs, located in the Kakuma refugee camp in Kenya, was facing difficulties joining us. Technological barriers in Kakuma made even primary participation a challenge. With no stable internet and limited power, connecting and being part of the summit seemed impossible.

The team and I were heartbroken at the thought of them missing out. The hub members had worked tirelessly, hoping to be part of the larger conversation and connect with others globally. "There has to be a way," we thought, refusing to let technology or distance defeat us. It was then that collaboration became our saving grace. We contacted the UNHCR, hoping they could help us bridge this gap. Together, we came up with a plan. The hub would have the necessary credentials to gather in the United Nations office, where they would have access to the internet and the resources they needed to join the summit. Finally, seeing them on the screen; their faces lit up with excitement, and a sense of triumph washed over everyone. This wasn't just about being able to join a call or the summit; it was about inclusion, about ensuring that distance didn't silence their voices, that technology will not set them apart.

That experience with the Kakuma hub didn't just end at the summit. It became a symbol, a reminder that while technology is powerful, the human spirit breathes life and purpose into it. Every moment and every connection we made reminded me that resilience, collaboration, and human connection could overcome almost anything. No matter how advanced our tools become, our spirit and determination will always be the defining factors. For every new technological barrier, there is always a way to make a path and ensure no one is left behind.

The journey wasn't just about getting everyone online. It was about finding ways to connect the unconnected even when the odds were stacked against us. It's easy to assume that technology alone can bridge the gap, but the truth is that technology is only as effective as the intentions behind it. Without leaders committed to equity, inclusion, and empathy, the digital world would be another realm of division, and it's already the case. We live in a world that constantly embraces technological advancements, but we must never forget the importance of intentional leadership to close geographical, economic, or social gaps.

Leaders must be agile and willing to navigate and overcome challenges related to digital inequalities. It's not just about throwing technology at the problem; it's about thinking critically and ensuring that the solutions we adopt are meaningful and inclusive. Technology can bring even the most remote and underserved communities into the fold when paired with a commitment to equity and access.

As the world continues its journey toward an increasingly digital future, we often overlook a hidden risk—digital exclusion. It's easy to assume everyone can access high-speed internet, the latest devices, or even reliable electricity, but that's far from the truth. According to Statista, only 66% of the world's population, have access to the internet in 2024. When we design community initiatives or pick collaboration tools, we must remember that true inclusivity means creating a space where everyone can participate, regardless of their location or resources. The human element in the digital age is not just about having access to the latest platforms or tools—it's about understanding that technology should serve all community members, not just those fortunate enough to have every advantage.

Leadership in this era of rapid change and innovation is about finding balance. There's no denying that technology will play an essential role in how communities are built, sustained, and scaled, but the human touch—the ability to empathize, connect, and inspire—remains irreplaceable. Technology should serve as a complement to our humanity, not a replacement. I feel strongly that at the heart of every thriving community lies something that no algorithm or platform can replicate: genuine connection. Trust, empathy, and shared purpose can't be programmed. They have to be nurtured, and it's up to us to keep them alive.

In the coming years, the leaders who will stand out won't merely master the latest tools or tech trends; they will be those who understand the limitations of these tools and embrace the human side of technology. They will be the ones who, in a world where digital tools are woven into every interaction, keep the human element as the driving force behind real connection and lasting impact. The future of community building, I believe, will belong to those who can see the whole picture—those who can harness the power of technology while never losing sight of the human connections that form the foundation of any meaningful community.

Thinking about it now, that day with the Kakuma hub taught me a valuable lesson. It showed me that the real strength of a community comes from the willingness to support each other, to find solutions, and to keep pushing forward, even when the path seems blocked. Every time I feel that pull toward the newest digital trend, I think back to that moment, to the determination on their faces. It reminds me to ask myself, "How can I use this technology to make real connections? How can I ensure that it serves everyone? Will everyone have access to this tool?"

Beyond access and inclusion, there's an even greater responsibility: ensuring that the tools we embrace do not deepen divisions, reinforce biases, or strip away the very essence of leadership and decision-making. Artificial intelligence, while promising immense potential, also carries risks. The systems we rely on are only as good as the data they are trained on, and without thoughtful leadership, they can reinforce inequalities rather than reduce them. AI-driven decision-making can prioritize efficiency over empathy, scale automation at the cost of human judgment, and inadvertently exclude those whose realities don't fit neatly into an algorithmic framework.

For instance, many organizations now use AI in recruitment, community moderation, and even leadership development. But what happens when these tools fail to recognize the nuance of human potential? When they perpetuate biases that overlook the very people we aim to uplift? Leadership in the digital age requires vigilance—an awareness that just because something can be automated doesn't mean it should be. It is our job to ensure that AI doesn't erode the fundamental values that communities thrive: fairness, inclusivity, and trust.

And then there's the shifting nature of work itself. The next generation of leaders won't just need technical skills; they will need adaptability, emotional intelligence, and the ability to navigate a world where AI and humans must collaborate. Jobs that don't even exist today will become the norm, but the defining factor of leadership will remain the same—the ability to bring people together, to create shared meaning, and to inspire action beyond what technology alone can accomplish.

This is where collective intelligence becomes essential. The future of leadership and community building will not be about individual expertise but about how effectively we harness the diverse intelligence of groups — how we create spaces where AI complements human insight rather than replaces it. AI can help us process vast amounts of information, identify trends, and even simulate solutions, but it cannot replace the power of lived experiences, cultural intuition, or the ability to read a room, adapt, and build trust in real time.

Technology alone doesn't bridge gaps. People do. When used thoughtfully, AI and digital tools can amplify impact, strengthen collaboration, and extend opportunities to those historically left out of the conversation. But that only happens when we, as leaders, ensure that technology remains in service to humanity, not the other way around.

That said, I remain hopeful about what AI can enable when guided by the right intentions. When built with inclusivity, fairness, and transparency at its core, AI can become a powerful force for good. It can help us decode complex challenges, personalize education for millions, and even drive solutions to the most pressing global issues—from climate change to healthcare through biogenetics for example. AI has the potential to expand human creativity, unlocking insights that might have taken years to uncover. It can foster deeper cross-cultural understanding, helping communities connect in ways that were once unimaginable.

If we are to build communities that thrive in this digital age, we must do more than just adopt the latest innovations. We must ask the hard questions. We must challenge the systems that prioritize speed over inclusion. And at the same time, we must embrace the opportunities AI presents to enhance—not replace—the human experience.

The real promise of AI lies not in what it can do alone, but in how we choose to wield it. If we can harness its power with wisdom, integrity, and purpose, then perhaps it won't be a tool of division but one of transformation. A tool that helps us create a future where technology strengthens our connections rather than weakens them—a future where no one is left behind, and where our shared humanity remains the foundation of everything we build.

I am sure that technology will continue to transform how we interact and communicate, but I'm equally sure that it will never replace the need for empathy, understanding, and compassion. These are the qualities that bind us together and that make our communities strong. No tool can foster trust or build relationships independently, no matter how advanced. Those are human tasks; as we move forward, we must keep that truth at the center of our work.

I hope the world will remember this lesson in the future. I hope the leaders who rise in this digital age will remember the importance of the human touch. They will recognize that while technology can make incredible things possible, our commitment to each other makes those possibilities worth pursuing. I realize that every challenge, every moment of frustration, and every setback is just another chance to strengthen those bonds and to prove that connection is stronger than any obstacle.

In this digital world, the tools may change, and the platforms may evolve, but the core of what makes a community remains the same. It's about people—about lifting each other up and making sure no one is left behind. As long as we hold onto that and keep the human element at the heart of our actions, I am confident that we will continue to build communities that are not only connected but truly united.

CHAPTER 20:
THE TECH TAPESTRY: WEAVING INNOVATION INTO COMMUNITY

"It has become appallingly obvious that our technology has exceeded our humanity."
– Albert Einstein

As mentioned in the previous chapter, technology has redefined what it means to build a community, pushing the boundaries of what community means. Through digital tools, communities expand beyond city or country borders, connecting individuals across continents, languages, and cultures. The fourth industrial revolution is in full swing, and its impact on communities, especially the ones with global reach, is undeniable. For leaders and community builders, the challenge now lies in adapting to this technological transformation while preserving the essence of human connection.

One of the most remarkable aspects of technology is how it erases geographical boundaries. In the past, communities were rooted in physical locations. People would meet, interact, and bond within a shared space. However, these boundaries no longer exist with the introduction of digital platforms. Now, people from opposite corners of the world can gather in a virtual room, engage in discussions, and collaborate on projects without ever meeting in person.

Accessible digital platforms such as Slack, Google Meet, Miro, and Zoom, or more sophisticated platforms like Salesforce or mighty networks have become the main channels for these interactions. These tools do more than facilitate formal meetings. They also create spaces for spontaneous, informal conversations—those quick check-ins or chats that make everyone feel part of something larger. During the COVID-19 pandemic, when physical meetings were impossible, these platforms became lifelines, sustaining the heartbeats of communities that could have otherwise drifted apart. Even now, as people gather in person again, these tools still play a pivotal role in bridging distances. They ensure that community members remain connected, engaged, and heard, regardless of location.

Beyond just communication, technology has reshaped governance and community management. Digital platforms now make it possible to collect data, report updates, and gather feedback in real-time. This openness and responsiveness are crucial in establishing trust and transparency. Communities, networks, or leaders can quickly gather members' input on decisions or projects, making sure the community's voice guides its future. It's fascinating how these real-time interactions build a sense of participatory governance, where everyone's ideas have a place. This way, a community doesn't just grow; it evolves based on the active involvement of each member. For leaders, these platforms provide an opportunity to be more responsive, adjusting and refining strategies in sync with the community's needs.

Then there's the emerging role of artificial intelligence (AI), which is quickly becoming an exciting development in community management. AI can streamline many of the operational tasks—things like scheduling, tracking memberships, or even handling resource management. When I think about it, the time saved is invaluable, allowing the community leadership to shift their focus to the more profound, strategic work of fostering connections and building a shared vision. AI-powered analytics also offer incredible insights into community engagement, helping leaders make more informed decisions. Trends in member participation or preferences become more apparent, making it easier to tailor activities or programs that resonate with everyone involved.

Yet, for all its potential, AI cannot replace the unique human elements that make a community thrive. Trust, empathy, and understanding are qualities no machine can replicate "yet". These threads bind people together, creating a sense of belonging beyond a platform or a tool. Leaders must remain vigilant, permanently anchoring their strategies in these human qualities, ensuring that technology enhances connections rather than replaces them.

Creating a community also means ensuring that technology is adaptable, accessible, and inclusive. Every time a new tool is introduced, it's essential to consider its usability for people of all backgrounds and abilities. I constantly remind myself that technology's purpose is to serve the people, not the other way around. If a platform feels intimidating or inaccessible, it fails its purpose. Leaders must check-in, ensuring no one feels left out or overwhelmed by the tech meant to bring us together. It's a delicate balance but necessary to maintain the true essence of community.

With the capabilities offered by digital tools, there's also the ability to build mechanisms for real-time feedback and interaction. In practice, this could look like a simple poll on a community decision or an open comment section where members can express their thoughts. It's a small gesture, but each comment, each bit of feedback, is a step toward making everyone feel involved. With these mechanisms, community members don't just think like participants—they become active shapers of the group's path forward. This is a powerful shift, one that turns a passive audience into an engaged and invested network. In a way, these digital tools give voice to each person, making it clear that every perspective matters.

AI is becoming more deeply embedded in communities' functions, offering even greater customization and insight. Yet, as much as AI can enhance efficiency, the leader's job is to ensure the community's heart remains centered on people. For instance, using AI to automate reminders or notifications can keep everyone informed. Still, the personal touch—a simple message of encouragement, a shared story, or a heartfelt thank you—builds a genuine connection—even that can be done by AI, but again, the intention is human. No matter how advanced AI becomes, the human touch is irreplaceable. After all, community is about connection, not perfection.

It's a balance—leveraging technology to support the efforts while keeping a firm grip on the values that make those efforts meaningful. The leaders who will excel are those who know how to use these tools and understand their limits. They will be the ones who bring people together through genuine relationships, not just polished platforms. As much as digital tools make things efficient, the best moments in a community often come from shared experiences, laughter, and vulnerability that technology can't manufacture.

In all of this, I keep returning to the importance of adaptability. Technology is constantly evolving, and so are the needs of a community. What might be the ideal tool today may no longer meet our needs tomorrow, and it's the responsibility of a leader to stay open to these changes, ready to adapt and explore new approaches while remaining true to core values. The best technology in the world means nothing if it doesn't genuinely serve the people using it. Every choice, every tool, and every strategy must come from a place of understanding—a recognition that the heart of any community is, and always will be, its people.

At the same time, as we lean on digital tools, there's a growing need for data protection and privacy vigilance. The more personal information members share through online platforms, the more we have to ensure it is safe. Leaders today face an essential duty to protect members' privacy, following regulations like the GDPR (General Data Protection Regulation), not only to meet legal requirements but also to foster a trusting environment. Transparency in handling data and providing members control over their information keeps a community strong and dependable in this digital age. Without trust, the foundation of the community can crumble, so handling data respectfully is crucial.

That being said, I see new and exciting technologies on the horizon that could reshape how communities interact and grow. Innovations like virtual reality (VR), artificial intelligence (AI), and blockchain have the potential to bring us closer in ways that once seemed unimaginable. VR, for instance, could create immersive environments where members from opposite ends of the world feel like they are in the same room, allowing for and establishing connections that feel tangible and real despite the physical distance. It's thrilling to imagine gatherings where geographical boundaries no longer matter, where people can feel part of something shared and unified.

Then, there's the potential of blockchain technology to offer more transparent, decentralized governance models. With its ability to securely record and verify transactions, blockchain could bring a new level of openness to community decision-making, giving each member an equal say and fostering a sense of shared ownership. But while the possibilities are exciting, these technologies are tools—means to enhance human interaction, not replace it. The purpose remains connection, not convenience.

Thanks to thoughtful technology integration, community building is becoming more resilient, inclusive, and connected. A leader's role will be to use these advancements wisely, creating spaces that empower every member to feel valued and included. By grounding technology in empathy and respect, communities can embrace the future while preserving the human essence that lies at their core.

Ultimately, it's not the technology that makes a community work; it's how it's used and the intention behind its application. Leaders of tomorrow will be those who can honor the human spirit that brings people together. A community's future is bright and filled with possibilities. But it's up to us to ensure these possibilities serve all members, enriching their lives and making them feel they belong.

PART 5:

FROM INDIVIDUALS TO IMPACT: LEGACY OF CONNECTION

CHAPTER 21:
ANCHORS OF LEGACY: ALUMNI AS PILLARS OF THE FUTURE

"Legacy is not leaving something for people. It's leaving something in people."
– Peter Strople

Alums are like the living roots of communities and can play a crucial role in their continuity, strength, and evolution. One critical thing I learned about maintaining this bond is that it requires intention. We can't afford to let relationships fade just because someone moves on. In our community, every member transitioning into an alum is another potential source of support, knowledge, and insight. As a Global Shaper and YGL alum, I have experienced firsthand how alumni can serve as pillars of support and bridges between generations, fostering a resilient network that adapts to change while upholding shared values and goals.

The role of alumni extends beyond mere involvement; it is about cultivating a lasting legacy that inspires active members and empowers the community. Alumni contribute not only through their experience and network but also by offering mentorship, guidance, and insights that shape the next generation of leaders. In the Global Shapers Community, for instance, alumni often return as speakers, advisors, or mentors, facilitating events and projects that foster growth and learning for younger members. Sometimes, they even come back to serve in the governance bodies. This legacy-driven approach is evident in practices like the "pay-it-forward" sponsorship system of the YGL Community, where alumni fund opportunities for current members to attend retreats or events that might otherwise be out of reach, such as the YGL Greenland Expedition, which is actually organized by an alum for the community to learn about the effects of climate change on territories such as Greenland. This tradition of giving back ensures continuity and reinforces a culture of mutual support. It embodies the spirit of community by encouraging each generation to invest in the next by bringing with them a wealth of perspectives shaped by years of challenges, growth, and success. Their insights are deeply valuable to the community, enriching strategic discussions with lived wisdom. But there is also a delicate balance to strike. Alumni involvement must remain supportive and unobtrusive, respecting the space for current members to take the lead. This means alumni step in only when invited by the current members or during designated mentorship opportunities, offering their guidance without overshadowing the actions of current members. It creates a respectful, intergenerational collaboration that preserves the autonomy of those currently driving the community's mission forward.

As Head of the Global Shapers Community, I often encountered the delicate tension between alumni passion and the need for them to release the reins. Many alumni find it hard to let go, feeling a profound attachment to the community they helped shape. I understand that pull—they still feel the pulse, the spirit, the exhilarating drive of the community within them. Yet, there is a risk in holding on too tightly and I faced this challenge, which, in some cases, became a conflict with some Shaper Alumni. If alumni are unable to release their hold, they inadvertently make it harder for the next generation to find their own path, explore new ideas, and redefine the community in ways that resonate with their own time and vision. It's a natural but challenging lesson, one rooted in love for the community—yet one that must be met with trust in the new leaders stepping forward.

As Global Shapers, I have seen the value of this approach, where alumni step back from daily operations yet remain engaged through digital platforms or by being there when needed. They often embody the values and traditions of a community, serving as a bridge that connects past achievements with future aspirations. In the Young Global Leaders community, alumni involvement goes beyond mentorship. They are encouraged to engage in projects that align with the broader mission of the community, from addressing pressing global challenges to advancing specific initiatives in areas like climate action or digital inclusion. Alumni thus play a dual role: upholding the founding principles of the community while helping it adapt to new global realities.

A significant aspect of this bridging role is seen during community-wide events, where alumni and current members come together, such as the annual Alumni Celebration Day in the Global Shapers Community or the YGL Summit. These gatherings are a space for sharing experiences, celebrating milestones, and envisioning the community's future, allowing alumni to contribute without assuming leadership roles over current members. It reinforces a continuity of purpose, reminding all members of the enduring mission that binds them.

While alumni are invaluable assets, it is essential that they create space for current members to lead and innovate. This principle aligns with the "constellation effect" in community building—a model where each individual, past or present, contributes their unique light without overshadowing others. Alumni are encouraged to guide and inspire, but they respect the autonomy and creativity of current members, stepping in only when their expertise is specifically needed. This balanced approach helps sustain an environment where each generation can understand the community's identity and impact without undue interference. I have found this balance rewarding.

It offers an opportunity to see how new members shape the community in ways that reflect their own experiences and aspirations. Being part of this continuum—where past efforts support current endeavors without dictating them—highlights the importance of adaptability and respect for each generation's contributions.

CHAPTER 22: **INSPIRING THE NEXT GENERATION**

"The best way to find yourself is to lose yourself in the service of others."
– Mahatma Gandhi

As I reflect on the kind of leader I aspire to be, the concept of servant leadership resonates deeply. In a rapidly evolving world where technology and social norms are in constant flux, leading through service and prioritizing others' needs feels more relevant than ever. Though not a new idea—championed by thinkers like Robert K. Greenleaf and James C. Hunter—servant leadership offers timeless principles that seem especially vital in our era, where community and connection are paramount. It shifts the focus from wielding authority to influencing and inspiring others while fostering an environment where people feel valued, respected, and supported.

Drawing on foundational insights from Greenleaf and contemporary scholars, I have developed the following definition, framed through my personal perspective on leadership:

Servant leadership is the practice of placing the growth, well-being, and empowerment of others at the center. It is rooted in humility, emotional intelligence, and the ability to build trust within diverse communities. Servant leaders prioritize the collective good, enabling others to reach their potential while creating sustainable systems where collaboration, inclusion, and innovation drive meaningful impact. It is not about authority or control but about fostering environments where everyone feels valued and inspired to contribute toward shared goals.

This approach feels like a call to action, a reminder that authentic leadership isn't about accolades or titles. It's about lifting others and ensuring everyone feels essential to a shared vision. In servant leadership, a leader's role shifts from being a figure of power to someone who removes obstacles and paves the way for others to succeed. When people see their leader genuinely cares about their well-being and growth, their commitment to the mission strengthens.

This approach is compelling in community-focused spaces, where people aren't driven by financial rewards or hierarchical obligations but by a shared purpose. I think about organizations like the Global Shapers Community or the Young Global Leaders. Here, people join out of passion and a desire to make a difference. In such settings, you can't lead by authority alone because people are here voluntarily, motivated by a collective cause. The power of a leader here comes from their ability to foster trust, inspire participation, and create a place where everyone feels they belong. It's about serving the community so it can thrive collectively.

Leadership today doesn't look like it did decades ago. We live in a time marked by globalization, geopolitical tensions, digital shifts, and rapidly changing expectations from younger generations. Millennials and Gen Z are drawn to authentic, transparent leaders who lead with humility. For them, leadership isn't about top-down control; it's about creating spaces for collaboration, making a positive social impact, and genuinely caring about people. My experience with the Global Shapers Community has allowed me to engage with some of the most dynamic young leaders of our time, predominantly from Millennial and Gen Z backgrounds. These generations bring new values, skills, and expectations into the workplace and into communities, redefining what they want from leadership. They are, in many ways, rewriting the rulebook.

In the context of servant leadership, this shift requires rethinking how we approach and inspire the next generation. Millennials and Gen Z expect more than traditional command-and-control styles. They seek leaders who stand for something meaningful, aren't afraid to show vulnerability, and are driven by purpose over profit. They want leaders who embody empathy, transparency, inclusivity, and flexibility.

Millennials and Gen Z have grown up in a world that constantly changes. Their defining traits—adaptability, tech-savviness, and a strong sense of purpose—stem from navigating rapid technological advances, economic fluctuations, and societal challenges from a young age. Unlike Baby Boomers and Gen X, who typically value structure, hierarchy, and clear expectations, Millennials and Gen Z thrive in environments where they can collaborate, innovate, and express themselves authentically. For them, work is not just about a paycheck; it's about meaning and alignment with personal values.

In the Global Shapers Community, I saw firsthand how Millennials and Gen Z hold purpose and growth as central pillars in their lives. They crave roles that allow them to make a tangible difference in the world. When presented with a task or a project, their first question is often *"How will this impact others?"* or *"How can this contribute to a greater purpose?"* They view their work as a platform for change and expect leaders who will empower them to explore, learn, and make that impact.

Gone are the days of rigid hierarchies and strict 9-to-5 workdays, especially for these younger generations. Millennials and Gen Z thrive in flexible settings that allow them to take ownership of their time and responsibilities. They are collaborative by nature and flourish in environments where feedback flows freely and where leaders and peers value their input.

In many Global Shapers hubs around the world, I observed how younger members preferred collaborative, non-hierarchical approaches. They often initiated cross-functional projects, bringing together diverse skill sets to achieve a common goal. To them, titles and formal roles mattered less than the impact and effectiveness of their contributions. They expect leaders who are comfortable breaking down barriers and who can create spaces where everyone's voice is heard and valued.

As a leader, embracing this collaborative and flexible mindset can be transformative. It means approaching projects as a co-creator rather than a director, showing trust by letting go of rigid structures, and allowing young talent to bring their ideas and creativity into the process.

Millennials and Gen Z are the most digitally connected generations in history. While Baby Boomers and Gen X might prefer traditional, structured communication, younger generations gravitate toward immediacy and authenticity. They're accustomed to messaging apps, video calls, and collaborative digital platforms, which enable instant, transparent interactions. For them, leadership is most credible when it is open and honest—when leaders forgo formalities (such as emails) and instead communicate with clarity and authenticity.

However, they often fall into the trap Simon Sinek described as instant gratification. This refers to the desire for immediate results and rewards without delay. As my little sister Laila aptly puts it—summarizing sentiments I've often heard from these generations—it stems from "a lack of trust in a system that once promised success over the long run but failed to deliver. We don't feel obligated to stick to society's standards, rules, or authority." This distrust has driven a strong preference for the here and now, where immediate action and outcomes are valued over deferred rewards. In the digital age, Millennials and Gen Z are used to getting things quickly—whether it's answers from a Google search, instant messaging app responses, or immediate entertainment access. This constant access to instant feedback and results can create a challenge in settings that require patience, long-term effort, and delayed rewards, like career growth or community impact. The expectation for quick results can sometimes clash with the slower, more sustained process of achieving meaningful goals.

I've also noticed that younger members resonated most when I shared not only successes but also challenges and vulnerabilities. They didn't want a leader who claimed to have all the answers; they respected a leader who could admit when they didn't and who was willing to learn alongside them. In servant leadership, this willingness to be transparent and vulnerable fosters trust and encourages a sense of shared purpose. It shows that the leader is there to serve the community, not to simply direct it.

Beyond purpose and impact, Millennials and Gen Z are deeply invested in personal growth and well-being. They expect leaders to provide opportunities for learning and development, clear pathways for advancement, and, crucially, an environment that prioritizes mental health. The younger generations are acutely aware of the importance of work-life balance, and they appreciate leaders who support a holistic view of success—one that encompasses not just professional achievements but also personal well-being.

In many ways, this expectation aligns seamlessly with servant leadership, which focuses on the growth and welfare of those being led. Servant leaders understand that for individuals to bring their best selves to work, they must feel valued, supported, and empowered. It means creating a culture where wellness programs, mental health support, and flexibility are prioritized. In Global Shapers hubs, I witnessed how leaders who championed well-being initiatives had the most engaged and committed teams. Younger members responded enthusiastically to wellness workshops, mental health resources, and flexible scheduling, seeing these efforts as signs of respect and care.

Anyone working with or leading younger generations—whether in hiring, collaborating, or community building—must recognize these evolving expectations. Millennials and Gen Z are not satisfied with traditional leadership models; they want to be part of a workplace or community that values their individuality, prioritizes well-being, and empowers them to create change. Servant leadership is uniquely suited to meet these needs, as it focuses on elevating and serving the team rather than controlling it.

I often find myself reflecting on how to cultivate these qualities in myself. What does it look like to lead with humility, for example? To put the needs of others at the forefront, even when it requires personal sacrifice? These aren't just abstract ideas—they're practical questions that shape how I engage with those around me. When I approach leadership as an act of service, I notice that people respond differently. A sense of trust builds, a sense of unity that strengthens when people see that their leader is just as invested in their growth as in the organization's goals.

Leading younger generations like Millennials and Gen Z requires this nuanced approach that aligns closely with their values. In reflecting on what I've observed, I realize that these younger members of our communities aren't just looking for leaders with capability; they seek compassion, authenticity, and empathy. They want leaders who offer meaningful feedback, foster personal growth, and instill a sense of purpose within the team. Servant leadership aligns perfectly with these values because it's rooted in the belief that a leader's role is to empower others and support their development. Leaders who listen, act with integrity, and guide with empathy naturally earn the trust and loyalty of younger members, which strengthens long-term engagement and dedication.

I often think about something Simon Sinek shared about the importance of empathy and long-term thinking. He highlighted the pressure on today's youth to achieve instant success and how this constant pursuit can lead to frustration and burnout. Sinek emphasized that leaders should balance the need for validation with patience, mentorship, and understanding—all qualities at the heart of servant leadership. Servant leaders have a unique opportunity to support young people through these challenges by fostering resilience, focusing on long-term goals, and offering a steady presence in a world that often demands immediate results. Additionally, they can empower the younger generation by encouraging them to voice their own solutions rather than being shaped by outdated rhetoric.

In volunteer-driven communities, this approach to leadership is essential. People in these spaces are motivated not by money or rewards but by a shared purpose and a desire to make a difference. Leaders here can't rely on authority or financial incentives to keep people engaged; instead, they must lead by example, earning trust and respect through consistent, compassionate actions. Communities like the Global Shapers thrive because they are built on trust and shared values. Servant leadership offers the framework to sustain that trust, ensuring every member feels valued, listened to, and supported in their mission to create positive change.

The reach of servant leadership is undeniable in both community and professional settings. It has become essential in workplaces where remote collaboration, flatter hierarchies, and emotional intelligence are increasingly valued. Managers and executives who prioritize their teams' growth and well-being are more likely to inspire loyalty, boost productivity, and nurture a positive work culture where innovation and creativity flourish.

As I continue this journey, I'm reminded that servant leadership is about embracing the people you serve. It's about making space for others to shine, giving them the tools they need to excel, and letting them know they are trusted. When people feel this support, they step up in surprising and inspiring ways. Watching a team member gain confidence, take ownership, or develop a skill brings a satisfaction that any personal accolade can't match.

The role of a servant leader becomes even more relevant in a rapidly changing world. Leaders must be adaptable, willing to shift perspectives, and ready to meet the evolving needs of those they serve. Technology, societal shifts, and global challenges demand resilient and compassionate leaders. Leaders can bridge gaps, foster understanding, and build stronger communities by focusing on service and adaptability.

Ultimately, servant leadership is a journey of purpose and growth. It's about laying down a foundation that will last, one that future leaders can build upon. I want to create a culture of empathy and empowerment, where leadership is not defined by one person but by a shared commitment to uplifting each other. This approach is about planting seeds, knowing that future generations will enjoy the fruits of today's work.

CHAPTER 23:
COLLECTIVE STRENGTH: THE CONSTELLATION EFFECT

"Individually, we are one drop. Together, we are an ocean."
– Ryunosuke Satoro

One of the most profound experiences of my tenure as Head of the Global Shapers Community was the journey of Sanju, a Shaper from Bangkok. Sanju had faced immense struggles with his mental health, carrying a weight that few knew about. He had battled suicidal thoughts for years and had even tried to take his own life multiple times. For him, this pain was isolating, a hidden struggle that he bore alone, unsure if anyone would understand. But as fate would have it, the Global Shapers Community would become the turning point in his life.

When Bangkok won the bid to host SHAPE Asia Pacific, Sanju found himself on the organizing committee, tasked with bringing together Shapers from across the region for an event that would inspire and unite. Organizing SHAPE gave him a renewed sense of purpose, a reason to push through each day. The community he found within the Global Shapers was unlike anything he had experienced before. Shapers rallied around him with unwavering support, not only helping with the event's logistics but becoming a network of friends who genuinely cared about him. In their presence, he felt seen and valued, his burden lightened just a little by the warmth and kindness of those around him.

During the event, Sanju confided in me about his struggles. I could sense that he needed to unburden himself, to share his story in a way that would allow him to feel less alone. I encouraged him to consider opening up to others, not just for himself, but as a way to inspire and connect with the community. There's a power in vulnerability that can be transformative, and Sanju's story was one that could remind others of the strength it takes to keep going, and the importance of leaning on those who care.

At the closing ceremony of SHAPE Asia Pacific, Sanju took a brave step forward. Standing before a room full of Shapers, he opened up about his journey—the struggles he'd faced, the darkness he'd endured, and the life-saving light he found within the community. His words moved the room, resonating deeply with everyone present. He was met with silence, not out of discomfort, but out of reverence for his courage. In that moment, Sanju wasn't just a Shaper sharing his story; he was a beacon of resilience, showing everyone the power of vulnerability and the life-changing support of a community that genuinely cares. He was our leader!

As he finished, the entire room rose in applause, and Shapers surrounded him in an outpouring of love and support. Sanju received the biggest hug of "ShapersLove," a moment of connection that I believe will stay with all of us forever. At that time, we were a beautiful constellation. It was one of the most rewarding moments of my time with the Global Shapers Community, a testament to the transformative impact of empathy and listening. Sanju's courage in sharing his story became a powerful reminder that, at the heart of every community, there is strength in showing up for each other, in being seen, and in finding hope through connection.

Building community through connection requires a shared vision—a guiding light for everyone to follow. This vision must be clear, compelling, and inclusive so everyone feels they have a stake in the community's success. When a vision is articulated, it needs to resonate with each person's values and aspirations, and people don't just follow a leader; they own the mission, working with purpose because they believe in what they're building together.

One of the most inspiring aspects of connecting individuals into a constellation is seeing the strength that diversity brings. When nurtured, diversity is a powerful catalyst for creativity, resilience, and growth. I've learned that a diverse group can solve problems in ways that a homogenous group might overlook. Different perspectives lead to more robust discussions, innovative ideas, and vital solutions. Diversity isn't just about including people from different backgrounds; it's about creating a culture where everyone feels free to bring their whole selves to the table.

In an interconnected world, diversity in leadership is vital. In a constellation, not all stars shine in the same way. When different perspectives are represented in leadership, it leads to decisions that are more reflective of the community. One of the challenges of building a constellation is maintaining alignment among individuals with different goals, backgrounds, and ideas. Alignment doesn't mean forcing everyone into a single way of thinking but instead finding common ground where individual goals support the broader mission. This takes patience, diplomacy, and an open mind. I often encourage open dialogues where people can voice their ideas, ask questions, and engage in constructive debates. These discussions help clarify our direction and reinforce the values that unite us. In these moments, I see how alignment and diversity can coexist, each enriching the other and strengthening the community.

Another aspect of the constellation effect is how it allows each person to grow and develop. Leadership isn't just about achieving objectives; it's about nurturing the potential within each individual. I take pride in mentoring others, guiding them not by telling them what to do but by helping them discover their strengths and capabilities. Mentorship within a constellation also works in both directions. I have learned countless lessons from those around me, from their insights, resilience, and creative approaches. Leadership is never a one-way street; it's a constant exchange where each person has something to teach and something to learn. This exchange is the lifeblood of any strong community, creating an environment where growth is mutual and continuous.

For the future, I see the constellation effect growing stronger as communities continue to diversify and expand. The key will be fostering connections that are not just functional but meaningful. Leaders must continue creating spaces for genuine interactions, ensuring each person feels they belong. This sense of belonging, of being part of something larger, is the heartbeat of any community. It makes individuals invest their time, energy, and passion into a shared purpose.

Connecting individuals into a constellation is ongoing and filled with learning, challenges, and triumphs. I am responsible for building those connections, helping others shine, and guiding the community toward a shared vision. The journey demands patience, empathy, and resilience, but the rewards are immense. I want to see people grow, see ideas come to life, and know that I played a part in creating a constellation that lights the way for others—this gives leadership meaning.

Leadership is about recognizing the brilliance of each individual and creating a space where that brilliance can come together with others to form something extraordinary. It's about nurturing connections, fostering trust, and guiding with humility. The constellation effect isn't just a theory; it's a way of leading that brings out the best in people, creating communities that are not only effective but deeply connected and resilient. As I look forward, I am inspired by the limitless potential of these connections, knowing that together, we can light up the darkest of skies.

CHAPTER 24: BEYOND THE SELF: THE POWER OF CONNECTION IN LEADERSHIP

"To go beyond is as wrong as to fall short."
– Confucius

Leadership, in its most accurate form, has always been about connection. The ability to link people, ideas, and purpose into a united force allows leadership to transcend personal achievement. The art of fostering connections transforms scattered ambitions into a shared mission, allowing individuals to tap into a larger purpose. Through my experiences, I've witnessed the incredible effect this has—like stars in the night sky that, when joined, form constellations. Each star holds its light, but they reveal something far more significant together. This is the essence of leadership: creating connections that allow people to achieve something that no single individual could accomplish alone.

In my journey with the Global Shapers Community and the Young Global Leaders, I understood how transformative these connections could be. I remember organizing events where we gathered individuals from diverse corners of the world, each bringing unique perspectives and talents. On their own, they were brilliant. But when they met, when they truly connected, something incredible happened. These weren't just meetings or conferences; they became moments of genuine transformation, where ideas sparked, bonds formed, and a shared sense of purpose took hold. Watching this unfold, I'd often say to my team, "Our goal isn't simply to inspire—it's to create powerful moments that touch each participant's core." Those connections became the real legacy of the events.

In these gatherings, I saw how deeply people craved belonging and purpose. Connecting with others on a shared journey taps into something bigger than we can imagine, igniting a passion beyond individual goals. When people come together and see themselves as part of something larger, they become motivated to take action. This idea of connected purpose, *The Constellation Effect*, became a guiding force in how I viewed leadership. It's not about rallying people around a leader but showing each person their role within the shared mission.

In moments of connection, barriers dissolve, and we see the world through new eyes. Mohammed's voice in Davos, for example, grounded in a reality most of the audience could only imagine, challenged people to rethink their perceptions. As he spoke, I saw eyes in the audience widen and nods of understanding ripple across the room. This was an invitation to shift perspectives, open minds, and embrace a reality that is often overlooked in rooms of privilege.

In a way, bringing Mohammed and others like him into these spaces redefines leadership. Leadership, after all, is not about who speaks the loudest or commands the most attention; it's about creating space for those with the most profound insights, those whose experiences hold truths that can reshape the future. By lifting voices like Mohammed's, leadership becomes a transformative force, pushing boundaries and challenging the status quo.

The logistical challenges of getting him to Davos were significant, but the impact of his presence there far outweighed them. From his first steps off the plane, Mohammed faced a series of new experiences. The feeling of stepping into a world vastly different from his own was part of the journey. Watching him navigate this new environment was a powerful reminder of what connection truly means. As he stepped onto that stage, I couldn't help but feel a sense of pride and anticipation. Here was someone who had been silenced by circumstances for so long, now standing in front of the most influential people in the world. And as he shared his story, he connected with the audience in a way that transcended words. It was clear that they were not just hearing him—they were feeling his journey, seeing his world through his eyes. At that moment, he was more than just a speaker. He was a bridge between worlds.

This is the true essence of the power of connection. Sure, it's about bringing people into a room together, but it's also about making space for each story, each voice, and each perspective to resonate. Connections can shift mindsets and inspire action. Mohammed's presence in that room transformed an audience of passive listeners into active participants, engaging them in a conversation beyond Davos's walls. The questions they asked afterward and the discussions sparked by his words were signs of a more significant and meaningful change.

The most purposeful impact of connection lies in its ability to inspire action. Mohammed's words moved people, not only emotionally but to the point of rethinking how they viewed global issues and their roles within those issues. By telling his story, he had created a shared sense of responsibility among everyone in that room. That's the true power of connection. It bridges gaps, creates understanding, and lays the foundation for meaningful action. Connection brings people together while also giving them a sense of purpose and belonging.

The collective power—this constellation of human potential—exists in every facet of life. From our families to our professional teams to our circles of friends, leadership is not about elevating a few stars but about creating a star team. It's about connecting individual talents to complement and elevate one another, making something more significant than the sum of its parts.

This is the power of a constellation. One voice inspires another, and soon, a collective momentum builds that can shift perspectives and inspire action on a global scale. I have seen this time and again in the Global Shapers.

Creating these connections requires intentionality. Uniting people is not enough; the real challenge is cultivating a space where each person feels safe and valued enough to share openly. When I organized events, I made it a point to start with exercises that built trust. For instance, a simple conversation about shared values would open the door to deeper discussions. Trust is the foundation, the unbreakable thread that binds people together, enabling them to express their ideas, even when those ideas are unconventional.

Connection creates resilience. When individuals feel isolated in their efforts, they are more likely to give up when faced with obstacles. But when they know they have the support of a community, their resilience grows. This sense of solidarity keeps people going, even in difficult times. In the Global Shapers Community, I saw this resilience often. People would face setbacks, but instead of giving up, they would turn to their peers for support and guidance. This support system became a source of strength, helping them overcome challenges that would have seemed impossible alone.

Beyond individual resilience, the power of connection also fosters collective courage. It takes courage to speak out, to challenge norms, and to push for change, especially on global stages where opposition is strong. But when people stand together, each person's courage reinforces the others'. This collective courage has been at the heart of some of the most impactful moments I've witnessed. The courage of young leaders standing together allowed them to speak honestly and boldly, even in front of influential figures. They knew they weren't alone, and that sense of unity gave them the strength to push boundaries and advocate for what they believed in.

In practice, this means focusing on human connection as the bedrock of any community or team. It's easy to get wrapped up in the logistics—budgets, deadlines, deliverables—but at its core, leadership is relational. It's about building trust, encouraging collaboration, and ensuring everyone feels seen, heard, and valued.

This is the essence of The Constellation Effect: bringing individuals together to form a collective force capable of extraordinary impact.

And this principle doesn't just apply to formal structures like professional communities or organizations. The Constellation Effect is equally powerful within our families, social circles, and informal networks. Communities don't need to be formal or structured to be impactful. They are made up of the people who support us, challenge us, and help us grow. As leaders—whether at home, at work, or in our social lives—we are responsible for nurturing these connections, ensuring that everyone feels valued and empowered to contribute. When we do this, we create a cascading impact that reaches beyond ourselves, transforming the lives of others in profound ways and leaving an enduring legacy of collective strength and unity.

This ripple effect is the natural beauty of connection—it reaches further than we could ever imagine. When people are connected meaningfully, they are inspired to share what they've gained with others, passing on knowledge, support, and encouragement. Connection becomes a chain reaction that touches individuals across borders and generations. It's this ongoing ripple that turns isolated acts into lasting change.

There's a kind of magic in watching this happen. I've seen it during events and gatherings where people from vastly different backgrounds and perspectives come together with a shared purpose. In these moments, people are not just learning from each other but forming bonds that motivate them to go out and make a difference in their communities. The initial impact of one person's story or experience spreads, influencing others who, in turn, pass it on. This ripple creates waves that can reach places and people we never anticipated.

This impact of connection extends beyond large gatherings and formal platforms. It's woven into daily interactions, the small gestures that often go unnoticed but profoundly affect someone's life. A simple word of encouragement or a listening ear can empower someone in ways we may never fully understand. It's in these seemingly small acts that genuine connection reveals its power. Whether in a room of world leaders or a quiet conversation, connection bridges gaps, fosters understanding, and inspires change. The small gesture that changed my life came unexpectedly, during a time when I was still finding my way at Al Akhawayn University in Ifrane. I was just another student, unsure of my path, filled with the usual doubts and insecurities that come with youth. I didn't see myself as someone who could lead or inspire; I didn't think I was "that person." But one day, Abdessamad Fatmi, the Director of Student Affairs at that time, pulled me aside. He looked me in the eye, and with a calm certainty, he said, "I see you as the next president of the Explorer's Club."

It was a simple sentence, but in that moment, it felt like a lifeline. He saw something in me that I hadn't yet seen in myself. Those words unlocked a sense of possibility I didn't know was there. They echoed in my mind, slowly chipping away at the self-doubt that had held me back. For the first time, I started to believe that maybe, just maybe, I was capable of leading, of making a difference. That small gesture—one quiet moment of belief—set me on a path that would ultimately shape my entire life. It taught me that sometimes, all it takes is one person who believes in you to ignite a spark that changes everything. To him, I am forever grateful.

I'm also reminded of the significance of connection in personal growth. Every person I've worked alongside has left a mark on me, shaping my perspective and enriching my understanding. The journey of leadership is one where those around us continuously shape us. Each interaction and story become a piece of the larger narrative we're all a part of. Leadership is about recognizing this shared journey and inviting others to walk alongside us, contributing their own stories, experiences, and insights.

Connections are the most essential foundation in building communities and networks. The thread binds individuals into a cohesive whole, turning a group of people into a powerful, unified force. Each person brings unique talents and perspectives, and when they are woven together, the result is rich, resilient, and capable of enduring challenges that might overwhelm any individual. Connection amplifies our strengths and creates a collective resilience that carries us forward.

Shared experiences, moments of understanding, and bonds of trust remind us of our shared humanity. Whether we're working toward social change, building a business, or simply supporting one another through life's challenges, these connections give our lives purpose and meaning. In this interconnected world, the role of leadership is to foster these connections, build bridges rather than walls, and create spaces where everyone feels empowered to contribute.

The journey of leadership, then, is one taken alongside others, where each person's contribution enriches the whole. In this journey, connection becomes the guiding light, illuminating the way forward and bringing people together in a shared vision. As I continue on this path, I am grateful for the connections that have shaped me and the opportunity to help create spaces where others can find their place within the constellation.

The power of connection is about transforming individuals into a force that can accomplish extraordinary things. This is the true essence of leadership, and it's a privilege to be part of it and to contribute to a world where connection is not just a byproduct but the driving force behind everything we do.

CHAPTER 25: **ILLUMINATING THE PATH FORWARD**

"Do not look where you fell, but where you slipped."
– African Proverb

The world needs leaders who focus not on themselves but on bringing people together. In this era of intense challenges—climate change, geopolitical tensions, deep divides within society, and growing economic disparities—the call for leaders grounded in empathy, connection, and service is more pressing than ever. This is a time for bridge builders, for those who can reach across differences, gather people into a shared space, and create an environment where every voice can find its place.

As I see it, the future of leadership is about finding a balance between honoring our roots and embracing the possibilities of what lies ahead. The values passed down from our families, communities, and cultures are the foundation, reminding us of who we are and the lessons that have shaped us. Yet, we cannot cling solely to the past. As a Shaper alum wisely said during our first Annual Curators Meeting, "As leaders, we stand on the shoulders of those who came before us, and now the question is, who will stand on ours?" We have a responsibility to create something bigger than ourselves. Leadership must dream beyond borders, both geographic and ideological, to create communities where people are empowered, supported, and heard.

Our issues are too vast in an interconnected world for any person, organization, or nation to handle alone. The future demands a different kind of leadership. It's about creating spaces where everyone has a seat at the table, ensuring voices from every walk of life are valued and included. The most urgent solutions will not come from a single individual or institution. They will emerge from a united effort, from the shared wisdom of diverse minds working in harmony. We foster these connections and open doors to meaningful change, creating a more just, equitable, and inclusive future.

Servant leadership gathers people into constellations of action, innovation, and resilience, creating a collective force that is far more powerful than any individual.

As I move forward, I hope this leadership approach—one that honors the past without being bound by it—will continue to grow. It's a vision of leadership that looks ahead to a brighter future but is grounded in real action and meaningful solutions. Imagine leaders as stars in a constellation; each shines in its own way, yet when they come together, they form something far more significant, brighter, and more potent than any star alone could create.

This vision of leadership, where individual strengths are unified into a greater whole, will guide us through tomorrow's complexities and uncertainties. It will build bridges across divides and create a world where everyone, regardless of background or circumstance, can contribute. This kind of leadership is needed to navigate our challenging times and create a more just, compassionate, and hopeful world.

The need for genuine human connection grows stronger in an increasingly virtual world, where technology often replaces face-to-face interaction. Technology may link us across miles but cannot replicate the trust that grows from a handshake, a shared laugh, or an honest conversation. I've witnessed this repeatedly, seeing firsthand how people are moved to action not by email threads or video calls but by the bonds formed through authentic, personal interactions. One of the most meaningful aspects of leadership in this connected age is creating environments where people feel valued enough to engage. When people feel this sense of belonging, they are willing to invest in themselves and are inspired to bring others along.

Problems like climate change, socioeconomic disparities, and digital divide are too vast for any person or solution. These challenges demand collaborative networks that combine diverse ideas, experiences, and skills. Over the years, I've dedicated myself to bridging divides, creating spaces for open dialogue, and building trust. The journey has shown me how powerful human connection can be when people approach it with open minds and hearts.

Reflecting on the path that led me here fills me with gratitude and optimism. Every challenge, every moment of doubt, and every shared victory has shaped my understanding of leadership. Leadership, I've found, isn't about perfection or personal accolades; it's about showing up, serving others, and embracing the unpredictable journey that leads to collective growth. This journey has shown me that actual community building reaches far beyond structures, governance, or even technological advancements. At its core, it's about human connection. It's about creating spaces where people feel they belong, can bring their true selves, and where the blend of diverse perspectives builds something far more significant than anyone could achieve alone.

Looking to the future, I know that communities must adapt to new challenges, incorporating emerging technologies and innovative strategies. However, the human element must remain at the heart of everything. Relationships, values, and shared goals are the threads that bind us, and no amount of technology can replace the bonds formed through trust, empathy, and shared experience. As leaders, we are charged with finding a balance between the digital and the human, the local and the global, the individual and the collective. This balance is where the future of leadership and community building will be defined.

This book reflects some of the many lessons I've learned along this path—a journey shaped by imperfections and humility. It's a collection of experiences, of obstacles overcome, of victories shared with extraordinary people who have joined me along the way. I hope these insights guide those passionate about leadership and community building and those who believe in the transformative power of human connection. Real change begins with each of us, and through our connections, stories, and shared experiences, we create ripples that extend beyond ourselves, transforming our communities and impacting the world at large.

Each of us carries a unique story, values, and dreams that shape who we are and how we interact with the world. Sharing our stories and embracing our journeys opens doors to deeper connections and builds stronger communities. This journey has shown me we can lead, serve, and make something far beyond our time. Ultimately, it's about the lives we touch, the communities we nurture, and the impact we leave behind.

CONCLUSION

Leadership is a journey. It's not something we're born with; it's a pathway we travel upon that deepens and transforms us through each experience, each moment of reflection, and each hardship we endure. Looking back at my journey thus far—from those early days as a student to navigating the complexities of global initiatives—I can see just how much my approach has been shaped by the people and communities I've been fortunate enough to connect with along the way. These connections, or "constellations," have significantly impacted my leadership growth, showing me that leadership is not about leading from the front. Instead, it's about serving others, fostering trust, and empowering those around me.

When I first stepped into leadership roles at Al Akhawayn University, I focused primarily on getting things done—coordinating events, managing projects, and ensuring goals were met. One of the critical moments that stands out is when we organized the Amazigh Days in conjunction with the Native Week. Bringing together the indigenous peoples of North Africa and North America to exchange cultures, languages, and stories, I saw how much more impactful the event became when people connected meaningfully. I will always cherish the discussions and learnings I had from Chief Robert TallTree and his wife Terri TallTree. Those conversations created something far more significant than I could have imagined alone. For the first time, I understood leadership was about building community and collective strength, not simply overseeing tasks.

These early experiences laid the foundation for my leadership philosophy. As I took on more significant roles, such as leading the Global Shapers Community and the Forum of Young Global Leaders, empathy and trust became central to my approach. I learned that leadership wasn't just about achieving results but rather about creating an environment where people felt safe sharing ideas, being vulnerable, and growing.

Leading the Global Shapers Community marked a defining moment in my journey, pushing me to adapt my leadership style. This role wasn't just about managing members, the team, or organizing events; it was about shaping a movement of young people from diverse backgrounds across the globe. Servant leadership, which had been a part of my approach, became a necessity. With a community as diverse and expansive as the Global Shapers Community, I realized it was essential to make sure every voice had space to be heard and that the platform we created is empowering others to lead, innovate, and make an impact. My decisions shifted from focusing on my own vision to asking what would genuinely serve the collective. I began to see my role as guiding each person to find their unique place in the constellation we were building together, making sure the entire community could thrive as one.

When people in the community felt disconnected or disheartened, leading wasn't about pushing harder or enforcing authority; it was about stepping back, truly listening, and figuring out what they needed most. Leadership doesn't always mean giving direction—it can mean being a shoulder to lean on, offering quiet guidance, or simply allowing others the space to step up. I came to understand that trust is the true currency of authentic leadership. In such times, I see how trust, once earned, could transform relationships and breathe fresh life into the relationships or the community.

Watching others grow is one of the most rewarding parts of servant leadership. When someone overcomes a hurdle or reaches a breakthrough, there's a quiet joy in knowing I played even a small part in their journey. Committing to servant leadership also means committing to fairness and equity. Recognizing that not everyone starts from the same place, I've focused on leveling the playing field whenever possible, making fairness a core part of what it means to lead by serving.

The sense of connection builds a kind of collective resilience that keeps us moving forward, even when times are tough. The Constellation Effect is not limited to formal structures; it's equally powerful within families, friendships, and informal networks. Communities don't need to be formal or structured to be impactful. They are made up of people who support us, challenge us, and help us grow.

As leaders, whether in our personal lives or professional roles, we have a responsibility to nurture connections that help everyone feel valued and empowered to make a difference. I'm reminded again and again that my greatest successes haven't come from personal achievements but from the collective impact of the communities I've had the privilege to support.

The network of relationships I've formed over the years has been the foundation of any success I've achieved. Leading with empathy and trust isn't a weakness; it's a powerful source of strength that allows us to create resilient, inclusive communities where everyone feels they have a role and a voice.

Servant leadership, empathy, and trust are central to my approach as I continue this journey. I have seen that leadership is not a solo endeavor but a collaborative effort in which the leader nurtures, guides, and empowers others. Leadership is a journey, and with every step, connection, and constellation formed, I continue to grow alongside the people that share the journey with me.

As you turn the final page of this book, I hope the path we've travelled together resonates deeply within you. The stories, the insights, and the moments of connection—these are not just pieces of my life but reflections of a universal truth: that real change begins with each of us. Leadership, at its heart, is not about standing above others but walking beside them. It's about lifting each other up, embracing our collective strengths, and finding purpose in our shared journey.

Each of us carries a light, a spark of potential waiting to ignite. When we bring that light into the world, we do more than lead; we create constellations of hope, resilience, and possibility. The constellation we form can light up the darkest of skies, illuminating paths we may never have found alone. Imagine what we can achieve when each of us steps forward with a willingness to connect, to serve, and to believe in something larger than ourselves.

In a world that often values individual success above all, I invite you to embrace a different path—a path where success is measured not by titles or achievements but by the lives we touch, the communities we build, and the impact we leave behind. Let us become leaders who value empathy, who build bridges, and who listen more than we speak. Let us become the leaders who inspire others to find strength in connection and to dream of a brighter, more inclusive future.

May this journey continue in your own life, as you take the spirit of connection and carry it forward. May you find purpose in uplifting those around you, comfort in the resilience of community, and fulfillment in knowing that the legacy you leave is one woven with compassion and understanding. Together, we can build a world where everyone's light shines, where every voice matters, and where our collective strength shapes a future filled with possibility.

Let this be our commitment—to lead with humility, to serve with heart, and to create a legacy that transcends us, leaving a world ready to shine even brighter for those who come after us.

BIBLIOGRAPHY

Ait Hamza, Mohamed. Et moi, dans tout ça...: Autobiographie d'un bledard. Rabat: Self-published, 2023.

Bennis, Warren. *On Becoming a Leader.* New York: Basic Books, 1989.

Brynjolfsson, Erik, and Andrew McAfee. *The Second Machine Age: Work, Progress, and Prosperity in a Time of Brilliant Technologies.* New York: W. W. Norton & Company, 2014.

Earl, Sarah, Fred Carden, and Terry Smutylo. *Outcome Mapping: Building Learning and Reflection into Development Programs*. Ottawa: International Development Research Centre (IDRC), 2001.

Goleman, Daniel. *Emotional Intelligence: Why It Can Matter More Than IQ.* New York: Bantam Books, 1995.

Greenleaf, Robert K. *Servant Leadership: A Journey into the Nature of Legitimate Power and Greatness.* Mahwah, NJ: Paulist Press, 1977.

Heifetz, Ronald A., and Marty Linsky. *Leadership on the Line: Staying Alive Through the Dangers of Leading.*Boston: Harvard Business Review Press, 2002.

Lexie, Pelchen. *Internet Usage Statistics In 2024*. Forbes. Mars 2024. Available at: https://www.forbes.com/home-improvement/internet/internet-statistics/

Hunter, James C. *The Servant: A Simple Story About the True Essence of Leadership.* New York: Crown Business, 1998.

Kegan, Robert, and Lisa Laskow Lahey. *An Everyone Culture: Becoming a Deliberately Developmental Organization.* Boston: Harvard Business Review Press, 2016.

Kohlrieser, George. *Hostage at the Table: How Leaders Can Overcome Conflict, Influence Others, and Raise Performance.* San Francisco: Jossey-Bass, 2006.

Kotter, John P. *Leading Change.* Boston: Harvard Business Review Press, 1996.

Mayne, John. "Contribution Mapping." *Evaluation* 7, no. 2 (2001): 179-192.

McMillan, David W., and David M. Chavis. "Sense of Community: A Definition and Theory." *Journal of Community Psychology* 14, no. 1 (1986): 6-23.

Schwab, Klaus. *The Fourth Industrial Revolution.* Geneva: World Economic Forum, 2016.

Senge, Peter. *The Fifth Discipline: The Art & Practice of The Learning Organization.* New York: Doubleday, 1990.

Sinek, Simon. *Leaders Eat Last: Why Some Teams Pull Together and Others Don't.* New York: Portfolio, 2014.

Sinek, Simon. *Start with Why: How Great Leaders Inspire Everyone to Take Action.* New York: Portfolio, 2009.

Scharmer, Otto. *Theory U: Leading from the Future as It Emerges.* San Francisco: Berrett-Koehler Publishers, 2009.

Tuckman, Bruce W. "Developmental Sequence in Small Groups." *Psychological Bulletin* 63, no. 6 (1965): 384-399.

Voss, Chris. *Never Split the Difference: Negotiating as If Your Life Depended on It.* New York: Harper Business, 2016.

Wenger, Etienne. *Communities of Practice: Learning, Meaning, and Identity.* Cambridge: Cambridge University Press, 1998.

World Economic Forum. *The Future of Jobs Report 2020*. Geneva: World Economic Forum, 2020. Available at: www.weforum.org/reports/the-future-of-jobs-report-2020.

Made in the USA
Las Vegas, NV
12 June 2025

f5d36bf2-029b-446a-b55d-88902067a9fcR01